MARGARET PRESTON

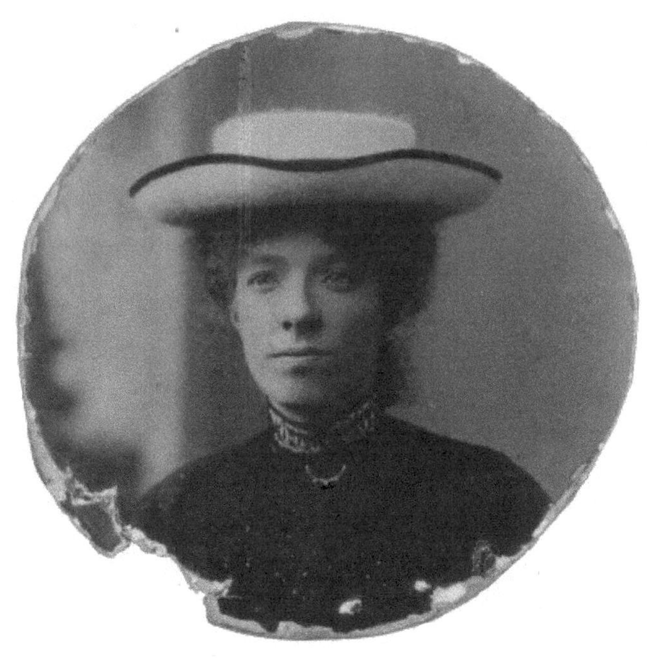

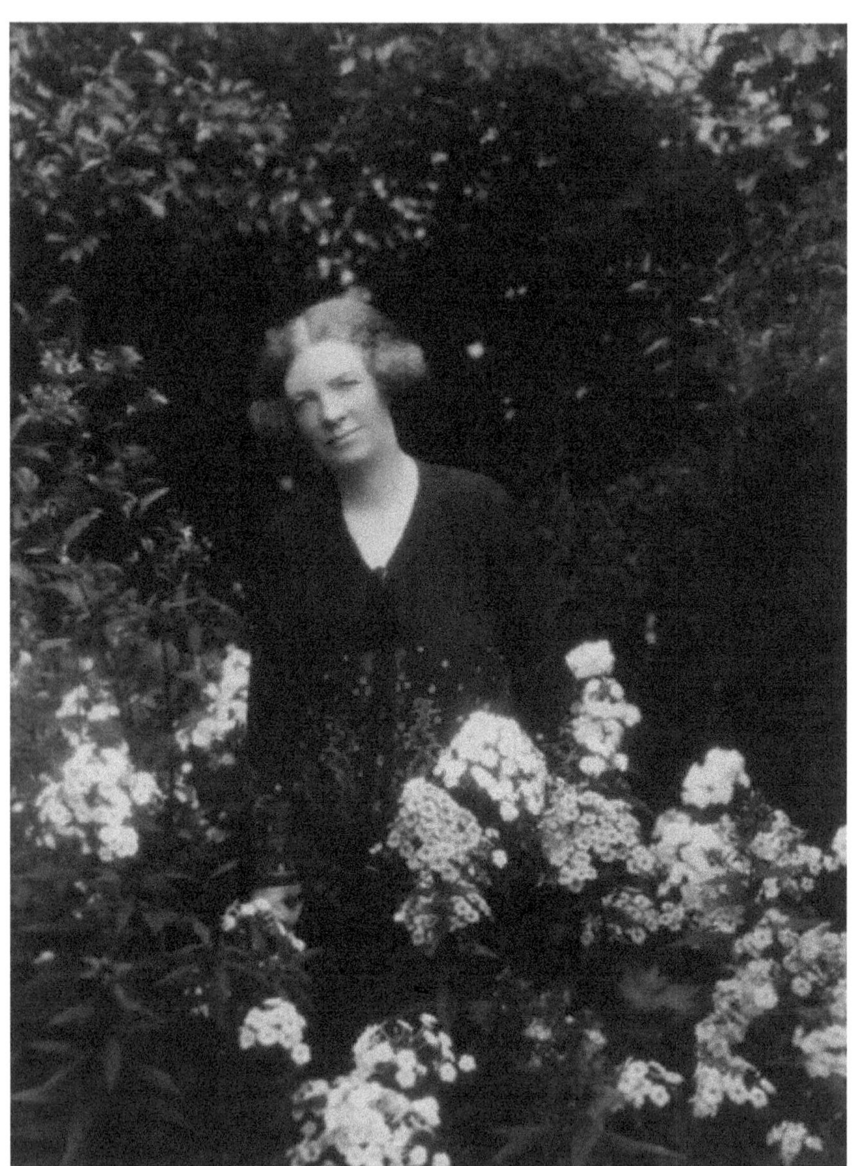

MARGARET PRESTON

ELIZABETH BUTEL

ETT IMPRINT, SYDNEY

This edition published by ETT Imprint, Exile Bay 2015

ETT IMPRINT
PO Box R1906
Royal Exchange NSW 1225
Australia

First published by Penguin Books 1985, reprinted 1986. Published by Viking Books 1986. Published by Penguin Books 1987, reprinted 1989, 1991.

Published by ETT Imprint 1995. New edition 2015.

ISBN 978-1-925416-01-5

The author is grateful to the Trustee of the Estate Late Margaret Preston, the Permanent Trustee Company Limited, for permission to reproduce the images and writings of Margaret Preston in all editions.

Design by Hanna Gotlieb

CONTENTS

INTRODUCTION

An artist is something on two legs with a simple soul and a belief that he was made before God — APHORISM 2[1]

Margaret Preston was Australia's foremost woman painter between the wars, a period when many of the best Australian artists were women. 'Their art was remarkably pure; painting was done for pleasure and from inner necessity, not often for money or for fame.'[2]

Talented, adventurous and certainly the most vociferous of the women artists, Preston differed from her compatriots in her strident demands for recognition – not simply for her own art but for the many theories she held about Australia's artistic atrophy. Her single, urgent plea was for a truly indigenous national art for this country, liberated from 'Grandpa G. Britain'[3] and the threat of internationalism, by a study of Aboriginal art. Her spirited crusade was partly the expression of her 'broad and bursting personality', as her friend Hal Missingham once put it[4] and also an outcome of the tenacity bred in her by experience.

Many of Australia's women artists from the early part of the twentieth century received financial support from their families and thus felt no pressure to compete commercially: `society permitted them to be artists but did not necessarily expect them to pay their own way.'[5] For Margaret Preston, the story was otherwise. Her itinerant childhood, from Adelaide to Sydney to Melbourne, ended in her mid-teens with a return to the city of her birth in 1894 for her sailor father's final illness and death. While studying at the Adelaide School of Design she began teaching to help support her widowed mother and younger sister, a career that continued long after the death of one and the marriage of the other. Preston submitted to the strain of teaching rather than compromise her art by painting pictures with one eye on the market. She wanted, as she wrote in 1927, to `paint her pictures as she would, to choose her own subjects and do them in her own way, leaving all thought of selling out of her mind.'[6]

Her determination to see where she stood artistically took her to England and Europe from 1904 to 1907, where her pride in her accomplished realism was shattered by coming face to face with modern European art, an experience she described in 1927 in `From Eggs to Electrolux.'[7]

> There in that horrid country no one seemed to understand Australian German, or appreciate Australian art. They were all hopeless. It was even worse for her when she found herself understanding in German what apparently sane artists and students were saying about a certain picture at a Secessionist Exhibition – a picture that had a large pink dragon, with a lady victim clad in yellow, being rescued by a gentleman in black clothes ... They were actually admiring it. It made her feel sick.

Overcoming her nausea she sought enlightenment through the study of Japanese art at the Musée Guimet and learnt `slowly that there is more than one vision in art.'[8] Her advances over her Australian contemporaries have, in part, been attributed to this study of the art that directly influenced Post-Impressionism, rather than to her analysis of Post-Impressionism itself. Returning to South Australia she resumed her teaching and her personal explorations, saving all the while `to be able to make a dash back to Paris to see if she had moved a little'.[9] This she did in 1912, consolidating her earlier lessons by an eight-year stay in Europe and England, which allowed her to experience the fierce, non-realistic colour and bold, apparently crude draughtsmanship of the Fauvists. Precision of design was now aided by the decorative possibilities of colour and she wrote to the painter Norman Carter from the Ile de Noirmoutier, a small island off the coast of France, south of Brittany, in 1913:

> I am very interested to hear of your decorative work – it is the only thing worth aiming at for this our century. It's really the keynote of everything – I'm trying all I know to reduce my still-life to decorations and find it fear-fully difficult ... now I know what you are exploring you can expect missives from me from time to time as I am more interested in this part of our Art than any other.'[10]

One look at Margaret Preston's invigorating, expressive and powerful art should convince the viewer that by `decoration' she meant something quite different from the vapid, artificial prettiness that has come to be associated with the term.

Living in England during World War I, she taught pottery and basket-weaving to shell-shocked soldiers at a military hospital on the Devon Moors, all the while developing her skills as a colourist. By the time of her marriage to William George Preston in Australia in 1919, she had been studying, teaching and experimenting with her art for almost thirty years. This late and financially secure marriage released her from the need to earn her living and allowed her full rein in applying her considerable energies and willpower to developing her art and her theories. Settling in Sydney where local modernism was a stylish, watered-down variant of the European revolutionary mode, Preston applied her aesthetic to interior decoration, fabric design and even flower arrangement, in addition to painting and print-making.

The Australia she had returned to was an urban society, but one which, nonetheless, still saw the landscape and pioneering traditions of the nineteenth century as its most appropriate visual expression. Depressed urban workers were led to believe that the bush was a place of healing away from the diseased life of the city. Furthermore, the bush was regarded as masculine in gender, a place to escape from the ladylike refinements of the city and women's challenge to supremacy, which had arisen through the freedoms that had come to them with the war.

Newly and happily married, freed from financial constraints and in complete command of the lessons she had learned in her years in Europe and England, Margaret Preston, in the full authority of her middle age, set about challenging the bush ethos and the entrenched traditionalism of Australian art. Her attack was vigorous, multi-faceted and sustained over the next twenty-five to thirty years. This book examines that attack through the rich variety of her vital art and the voice of the artist herself, in her writings and theories. These come to us today, over half a century later, ringing with the conviction of a fresh, original mind.

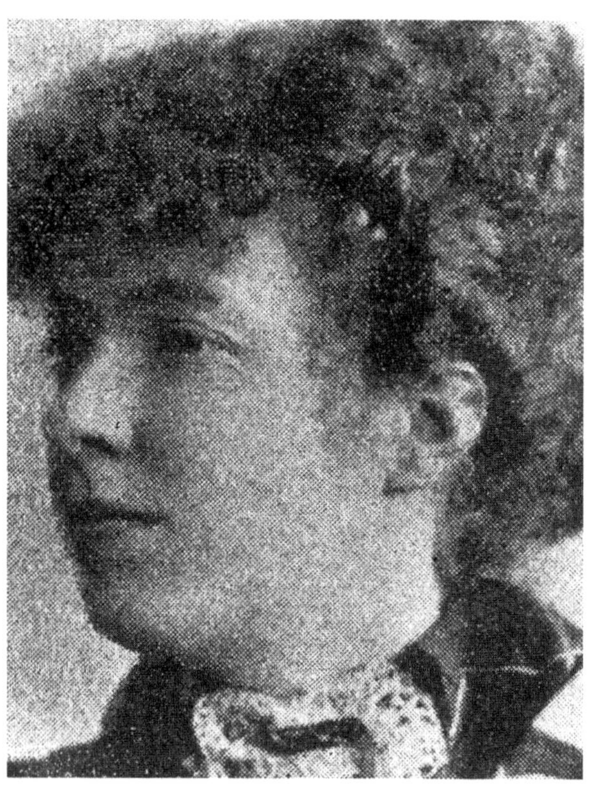

1875–1920

A lemon can be an inspiration as well as a fruit — *APHORISM 53*

Margaret Preston used still-life as a subject throughout her career but her greatest achievements in the area coincide with her first period as a mature artist between 1915 and 1930. This could be said to start with Summer, 1915, painted when the artist was still Margaret Rose MacPherson[1] and had been living in France and England with her friend, the South Australian potter, Gladys Reynell, for over three years.

The early understanding gained from Japanese art at the Musée Guimet on her first trip to France in 1904, was now injected with the tonic of Post-Impressionist colour, which she rhapsodized over in a letter to the painter Norman Carter in the summer of 1913:

> Please do not think me impertinent if I give you a few notes on what I've seen lately at the shows in the way of Décor – I went to one only for Décor – the most beautiful thing there was by a man called Gauguin. It was painted in Tahiti – a Virgin Mary with a baby – it had the dense purple of the island hills at the back, queer green banana tree foliage on purple earth – the Tahitian woman dull ochre holding the Christ, a blot of

ochre – two figures in the shadow of a tree, dull yellow and pink and in the foreground, melons and banyans in shadow – every colour every line helped to balance each other. It was only small but so sure…[2]

She was thirty-eight years old and had already proved herself to be a woman of intrepid spirit, devoted to her work and ready, when necessary, to slough off old ideas and old methods. Clearly she experienced one of those personal revolutions that sometimes graced the adventurous during those years in Europe and England and broke through 'the umbrous gloom' (as Robert Hughes puts it)[3] of her earlier work, to a stinging, vibrant new vision of reality. She transcended the meticulous and stolid art of her student years and henceforth, colour, flat patterning and dynamic line combined in her work with a boldness and drama, second only to the personality of the artist herself.

Why there are so many tables of still-life in modern paintings is because they are really laboratory tables on which aesthetic problems can be isolated —APHORISM 46

Margaret Preston had been solving her aesthetic problems on the tables of still-life since 1888, when, as a girl of thirteen, she studied painting under W. Lister Lister at his studio in Sydney's Angel Place. According to her autobiographical essay, 'From Eggs to Electrolux',[4] her first still-life was a picture of a striped tablecloth with a studio pot.

She was born Margaret Rose McPherson, on 29 April 1875, at Port Adelaide, to David McPherson, Scottish marine engineer, and Prudence McPherson (née Prudence Cleverdon Lyle), her Quaker mother. Her sister, Ethelwynne Lyle McPherson was born two years later. As with many women of her generation, her first name Margaret was probably a gesture to social or family tradition and for all practical purposes, she was called by her second name, Rose. In 1885, the family moved to Sydney where she attended Fort Street Girls' School, leaving about two years later to begin studying art. By her husband's account, she left school on the advice of her headmistress, to take private art lessons because 'she was much more interested in drawing than in her lessons',[5] but in her writings of 1923, she tells the story somewhat differently:

> Once upon a time when I was twelve years of age I borrowed (?) my mother's best dinner plates and brunswick blacked them all over. On to the blacking I painted flannel flowers. The result so impressed my mother that after the shock of the loss was over she determined to have me properly trained. Her justification was that as the flowers were the image of the natural ones I must have talent.
>
> `Why I became a Convert to Modern Art'[6]

Four years later, she was telling the story differently again in an autobiographical essay that, in its use of the third person separated her fifty-two-year-old self from the young girl who had first visited the art gallery forty years before:

> She remembers quite well her excitement on going through the turnstile to be let at large in a big, quiet, nice-smelling place with a lot of pictures hanging on the walls and here and there students sitting on high stools copying at easels. Her first impression was not of the beauty or wonder of the pictures but how nice it must be to sit on a high stool with admiring people giving you `looks' as they went by . . . This visit led her to decide to be an artist. Her mother, being persuaded that she wasn't fit for anything else, asked advice from the school teacher, who recommended a needy friend.
>
> `From Eggs to Electrolux'

Lessons in china-painting followed and then her classes with W. Lister Lister: `and let me tell you he was a very nice-looking, charming young man.'[7] The time reference of the descriptions was the same and possibly the incidents coincided, but Preston seemed to shape her articles in much the same way she might design a picture – flattening the perspective and introducing patterns or rhythms that would benefit the overall structure, and not simply represent reality.

It was Lister Lister, it seems, who eventually persuaded her mother to take her to Melbourne `to learn, in a big school, with other students, how to draw from the antique, to begin at the beginning.'[8] With her father being at sea so much of the time, it did not make much difference to others in the family where they lived, and so they went to Melbourne. In her essay, Preston implies that the move took place immediately but, in fact, it was five years before she began her studies at the Melbourne National Gallery School, at that time, the most prestigious institution of its kind in Australia.

She began drawing lessons with Fred McCubbin – `one of the kindest, cleverest artists Australia has produced'[9] – and appreciated the freedom he allowed her. The precocious abilities that had impressed her mother stood her in good stead and she shared second prize for drawing the full figure from the cast, for which she received a term's free tuition. Her studies were interrupted in 1894 by the illness of her father, who had been admitted to Glenside Asylum, Adelaide, for `Imbecility', aged forty-two. Margaret returned to Adelaide to be of support to her mother and remained there for two years, during which time, David McPherson died from `General Paralysis of the Insane', or tertiary syphilis. This was not so uncommon a fate before the 1940s, due to the difficulty of early diagnosis and the lack of effective treatment.

This experience must have been extremely traumatic for her and her family and could have influenced Margaret's decision against an early marriage. But from every record she has left, Margaret Preston was not a morbidly introspective person and when, in 1896, she returned to Melbourne to study under Bernard Hall, director of the gallery and head of the art school, she resumed her training with the same single-minded dedication as before.

Her portrait of Bernard Hall, well known as a disciplinarian, was respectful:

> He was certainly the finest teacher she ever had; every student respected and feared him . . . But wasn't he vitriolic! Nerves of iron and talent were necessary to stand his onslaughts, especially to one who could not appreciate his liking for hideous models.
>
> `From Eggs to Electrolux'

Under Hall, Preston progressed from charcoal studies of plaster casts to drawing from the nude model. By a combination of prevarication and good luck she often managed to escape the leaden atmosphere of the life class. Hall had a system whereby students drew numbers to determine their placement around the model. Margaret seems to have always drawn the last and therefore worst place, thus allowing her to leave the crowded class and work quietly at still-life in an adjoining studio.

> Here she would work day in and day out, at her precious eggs etc. Often many days would she spend painting at a small, high light, such perfection of detail being demanded.
>
> `From Eggs to Electrolux'

Her diligence again paid off and she won a further drawing prize the next year, 1897 – the still-life scholarship, as she called it. `It would seem that a liking for the colour and form of inanimate objects was born in her,'[10] she commented. The Argus of 17 December that year records the honourable mention that Miss MacPherson received in the still-life category of the National Gallery School awards, and the judges' satisfaction that this subject had been introduced into the curriculum of the painting school. In 1898, she returned to Adelaide where she continued her studies at the Adelaide School of Design, under H. P. Gill. There, she attended life drawing class with Hans Heysen and, released from the ballot system that had operated in Melbourne, she sat as close to the nude model as possible, an impertinence that led the twenty-one year-old Heysen to regard her as a `hussy'.[11] Despite her growing devotion to still-life and earlier dislike of the life class, it was clear that she would take every chance to develop her skills that was offered to her.

Leon Gellert, one-time joint editor of Art in Australia, recalled Preston at this time as

> a lively red-head who had figured prominently at the Adelaide School of Design during the days when I attended elementary classes conducted by the pompous and rather objectionable principal, Harry P. Gill. She was either an advanced student or an instructor of some sort.[12]

Stella Bowen, later a pupil of Margaret Preston's, has left a description of the School of Design in her autobiography, Drawn From Life. There she learnt to draw cubes, cones, pots, scrolls and plant life. The still-life groups they were required to paint were a curious and precious mix of objets, `a fan, a slipper, and a string of beads, or a vase with a peacock's feather stuck in it and a satin bow tied round its neck'.[13] William Preston was under the impression that Margaret began teaching at this time, to provide for her mother and younger sister, or at least to supplement the income. This impression is reinforced by comments Margaret made in a 1931 interview with Woman's Budget:

> When I was a young student and teacher ... I did still-life and landscapes. Chiefly the former because after a hard week's teaching I had not the energy to go tramping round the country with my gear, looking for a paintable spot. Also, I had a house which required supervision ... and still-life is essentially a woman's work from that point of

view, if from no other. You can go on working, even in the kitchen, if need be, and seeing to the things of the house while your work grows. Many of my pictures have been done in the kitchen with one eye on the stew.[14]

The following year, in 1899, Preston established her own classes in a studio in the A.M.P. Building in King William Street, Adelaide. She continued to teach for the next five years; financial independence gained, she could develop along her own lines. She wrote:

> Her art work really began at this time. It shows a movement of thought which is continuous throughout ... Against all opposition of friends and relatives she painted eggs, dead rabbits, onions – just everything she liked. It was no use for her to explain to people that the standardised beauty for art of landscapes, sunsets and ladies did not interest her ... So, she simply didn't try.
>
> 'From Eggs to Electrolux'

In 1903 Prudence McPherson died and a year later Preston was on the boat for Europe, accompanied by Bessie Davidson, four years her junior and one of her students at the Adelaide studio. They were bound for Italy, Germany and France – and an extraordinary awakening for two young women from drowsy Adelaide. Preston would return to Europe and England for an extended stay and Davidson would eventually make her home in Paris, serving with the French in World War I and as a member of the French Resistance during World War II.

The death of her mother released Preston from her Australian bonds at a crucial stage in her development. As the elder daughter of an exclusively female family unit, whose developing talents took her mother and sister from one capital city to another, she must early have formed a strong sense of responsibility and independence – not to mention the fabled egotism that threatened to overtake her in later life. From all Preston's writings it is clear that her mother made Margaret's artistic training a priority, even to the extent of making her sole beneficiary of her estate (William Preston believed that her sister married at this time). Mother and daughter must have formed close ties, with David McPherson away at sea so much of the time, ties that could only have deepened during the crisis brought on by his illness and death. But leaving Australia had become an imperative for Preston, for her explorations at the weekends, away from her teaching, had begun to worry her. She wrote in `From Eggs to Electrolux':

> her ideal at this time was to paint [eggs or rabbits] with such fidelity to nature that they could almost be used in the kitchen. As soon as she saw her hopes likely to be realised, her mind worried her. If she really painted as well as that, surely she would be the best painter of still-life in the world. The doing of it was so easy. It was this fact that raised a doubt in her mind about her possible fame; so, being orphaned, she started to put by pence until they became pounds, to take a trip abroad to see really where she stood and also to get some `finishing' lessons.

As it turned out, it was more a question of `starting' lessons than of `finishing'. In an article for The Home magazine in June 1923, `Why I became a Convert to Modern Art', she lamented the `imitativeness' of her early training, with its classical, tradition-bound ideals.

> Would that I could have had the advantages offered by the Slade School in London where the sculpture of the Greeks and Co. flourish in museums and not in a live school, and where all imitativeness is discouraged.

Bessie Davidson's parents were very much against the impropriety of the two young women making Paris their base, so they settled upon Munich, intending to stay there for two years. Preston could not work up any enthusiasm for the paintings they saw, en route, in Venice, for, as she wrote, `to the pure all is pure, to the blank all is blank'.[15] In Munich they took lessons briefly at the Government Art School for Women, with the services of a translator. The little Australian has excellent observe,' a distinguished professor there remarked.[16] They visited the Secessionist Exhibition, where Gustav Klimt and others were on show and Preston found herself becoming more and more frantic in her efforts to understand. The Secessionists were an independent, anti-academic group in which artists, architects and designers were united by their interest in Post-Impressionism and Art Nouveau and Preston later commented:

> My letters about this time written back to my native country could be compressed into a few sentences such as: Half German art is mad and vicious and a good deal of it is dull; I am glad to say my work stands with the best of them.[17]

This brash assertion cloaked a growing confusion, however, and the pair left for Paris, seeking enlightenment at the risk of their morals. `Alas! for all her hopes' Preston later wrote of herself.

The Autumn Salon was just closing, but she found this show exceeded the outrageousness of the Secessionists. Under these disturbing conditions there was only one thing to be done – to get a teacher who was a moderate and yet intelligent, to explain and teach what these people thought they were doing. The first thing this wise man did was to realise that our little Australian was really worried and wanted to learn. So he sent her to study Japanese art at the Guimet Musé, to let her learn slowly that there is more than one vision in art. That a picture could have more than eye realism. That there was such a thing as aesthetic feeling. That a picture that is meant to fill a certain space should decorate that space . . . That each century should have some of the characteristics of itself in its art. All this and so much more that our poor little artist was obliged to become a very humble student indeed. She found that she had been hopping about on one rung only of the ladder of art. Starting off again she tries to add another quality to her realism – that of decoration.

'From Eggs to Electrolux'

Preston had 'bad growing pains'[18] as she put it, but in the following two years she learnt her lessons well, studying in Paris and travelling in Spain, Holland and Italy, learning 'to appreciate the mighty qualities in the works of these countries'[19] and exhibiting work at the Paris Salon of 1905. Her study of Japanese art, under 'one of the leading teachers [of design] in Paris' as she commented in 1931,[20] awakened her to a range of qualities that became evident in her later work. Some of these qualities were: a delight in asymmetry; pattern as a dominant element of design; the close-up observation of natural patterns so that they are revealed in discrete units; the celebration of the uniqueness of particular flora; pleasure in the small event, making the unimportant emotionally and aesthetically significant; and a daring engagement in a deliberate primitivism. These characteristics did not become evident until she had gained some mastery of colour but in 1931 she paid tribute to this time, saying, 'my present work is the result of that training'.[21]

In 1907 the two women returned to Adelaide and leased a studio in the Steamship Building, in Currie Street, holding a joint exhibition in March of the same year. Thus far Preston had exhibited annually, when in Australia, with the South Australian Society of Arts and in the yearly Federal Art Exhibition held at the Institute Building, Adelaide. Her European sojourn had increased her confidence, and that year her painting Onions was purchased by the National Gallery of South Australia.

Her friendship with Bessie Davidson was something of a prototype for the two other important relationships in Preston's life – her friendship with the potter Gladys Reynell, and her marriage to William George Preston. Apart from sharing a professional relationship with Davidson, she apparently lived in the Davidsons' house in Prospect for two years, having been invited for a weekend 'sometime before 1910', as Sybil de Rose, a niece of Bessie Davidson, remembers. Ms de Rose's father, who referred to Preston as 'that red-headed bitch',[22] also epitomizes a number of men, both within the art world and out-side, who were less than admirers of the artist at different points in her life. It has been suggested that 'she looked for stronger figures to associate with'[23] and Preston does seem to have thrived on an intimate, supportive relationship, firstly with her two close women friends and later with her husband. She travelled extensively with all three and all three were younger than her, Davidson by four years and the other two by six years. Perhaps rather than seeking 'stronger' figures, she sought to balance her own strengths with individuals who looked up to her but who also possessed quiet reserves that she could draw on at times.

All three had financial resources that were occasionally (or in the case of her husband, consistently) of benefit to her, but there is nothing concrete to suggest that this was a dominant factor in her relationship with them. Given the rarity of Preston's dogged independence in her early years of teaching in Adelaide, it would only have been young women of some financial means who would have had the freedom to accompany her on her journeyings.

She resumed her teaching, both of private students and of classes at the Presbyterian Ladies' College, St Peters. Bessie Davidson's departure for Paris in 1910 saw Preston move to a new studio at the Commercial Bank Chambers. She defined her aim at this stage as

> trying to find her feet for her new movement – the addition of design in colour to realism. But now how difficult are friends and relatives, and so inconsistent. Only a few years ago they were grumbling because she would paint such horrid subjects as dead rabbits and fresh eggs. Now they were complaining because she is painting large gay flowers against gay backgrounds . . . For two years she experimented in colour, searching

always to get an aesthetic feeling in her work, and all the time penny-piling to be able to make a dash back to Paris to see if she had moved a little.

`From Eggs to Electrolux'

Her reputation was growing and a commission came from a Citizens' Committee to paint a posthumous portrait of Catherine Helen Spence, the Adelaide social reformer. Preston's pupils in 1911 included Stella Bowen, a painter who later shared a nine-year association with Ford Madox Ford, by whom she had a daughter. In her autobiography, Bowen sketches a portrait of Adelaide at this time which casts light on Margaret Preston's later attitude: `glorious Adelaide. Let's leave it at that.'[24]

I wish I knew the truth about that strangely dim and distant life in Adelaide before the war. I have reconstructed it in my memory as a queer little backwater of intellectual timidity – a kind of hangover of Victorian provincialism, isolated by three immense oceans and a great desert, and stricken by recurrent waves of paralysing heat. It lies shimmering on a plain encircled by soft, blue hills, prettyish, banal, and filled to the brim with an anguish of boredom.[25]

For Bowen, one of the few stimulating individuals in Adelaide was her art teacher, Miss Rose MacPherson, to whose studio she went two days a week. As Bowen describes her, she was `a red-headed little firebrand of a woman who was not only an excellent painter, fresh from Paris, but a most inspiring teacher.'[26] The MacPherson studio in the city was probably one of the few in South Australia to employ a nude model and given Preston's earlier aversion to Bernard Hall's `hideous models', it is not surprising that her choice was `only a little girl of 14'.[27] She had about twenty pupils at this time and set about teaching them to paint through the study of tonal values, an extension of her early training, rather than of her more recent discoveries in Paris. She did, however, encourage them to make a direct attack upon the canvas and through her `knowledge, integrity and dynamic enthusiasm', as Bowen put it, `did wonders in setting all my machinery in motion.'[28]

Gladys Reynell was also a pupil at that time. She was the grand-daughter of John Reynell, who had come to South Australia in 1838, planted vines and started winemaking at Reynella. Gladys was born there in 1881, the youngest of five children, becoming `a very beautiful woman, rather large and with black hair and dark blue eyes like all the Reynells.'[29] After Bessie Davidson's departure, Reynell took her place in Margaret Preston's life. In February of 1912 they left for London together on the S.S. Ascanius, with Paris as their final objective. The summer of 1913 found them on the Ile de Noirmoutier for four months, a vantage point from which Margaret wrote to Norman Carter of their plans:

> We (Miss Reynell and myself) are going to London at the end of this vacation. I'm very keen on trying to show at some of the small shows in London and having exposed three times in Paris and at a fair number of small shows there, feel I can still send to the Salons and explore other fields...[30]

The letter conveys her excitement at the work they had been seeing. The `decorations' of Aman Jeans[?]; a Gauguin painting of Virgin and Child; and Brueghel – `(the younger devil)' – whose work they had seen in Basle, `(we walked there over the mountains of Alsace Lorraine to see the Holbeins)'. She advises Carter to be sure to see `the Decorative Musée in the Louvre – quite apart from the painting Louvre' and gives her address in Paris as 64 Rue Madame.

Preston's interest in Gauguin (in the 1920s, with her husband, she followed his path across the Pacific on a journey of personal exploration) is revealing. Gauguin's early appreciation of the austerity of Breton life, with its crude religious sculpture based on old Celtic design, was united with a use of colour raised to the greatest possible intensity of pitch. In this way, decorative effect became charged with feeling. Later, in his paintings of native life and the landscapes of the South Seas, these elements were woven to Polynesian folklore and symbols. It does not take a close inspection of Preston's work to notice the similarities, both in the sumptuous colour of her still-life and woodcuts, and in the austerity and primitive dignity of the Aboriginal-inspired paintings of the 1940s. Cézanne regarded Gauguin as a mere painter of silhouettes and this edge between essential structure, as defined by Cézanne's spheres, cones and cylinders, and form described by line became a preoccupation of Preston's.

The Paris correspondent for the Melbourne Argus, in June 1913, noted the presence of a Miss MacPherson picture at the Salon; `The

Balcony in November: Still-Life ... nothing melancholy in the fruit and plates pleasantly painted in quiet silver light'. Leon Gellert later bought one of the works from this period – Still-Life 1913 depicting an alfresco luncheon, complete with wine, flowers and coffee pot, all on a checkered tablecloth. 'Actually, the artist herself regarded the picture ... as a purely period piece of her development' he wrote in 1967, 'executed when she was experimenting in the Impressionist manner.'[31] At this stage Preston had introduced a genre element into her still-life, with a casually placed chair suggesting imminent occupation and a patch of garden and a rustic gate in the background. Soon she was to abandon any anecdotal references and focus purely on the 'laboratory table' of the still-life itself, harvesting a series of richly decorative and technically adventurous images throughout the 1920s.

While living in Paris circumstances arose that led Preston to change her signature, from Rose MacPherson to Margaret MacPherson. An earlier habit of using McPherson and MacPherson interchangeably compounds the confusion, which, when her married name, Margaret Preston, is added, gives several signatures in all. This multiplicity of names has been interpreted as an attempt to hide behind different identities, but the artist herself gave a far more prosaic explanation in the interview with Woman's Budget in 1931:

> I had been teaching in Adelaide for some years under the name Rose MacPherson, though my full name was Margaret Rose MacPherson. When I went to Paris there was continual misunderstanding with the banks because I signed Rose MacPherson and at the request of one banker I began to sign Margaret MacPherson. The question arose 'Could I succeed as well under a new name as under the one by which I was so well-known?' and I decided to put that to the test.

Margaret Preston liked 'tests' and consistently challenged her own artistic preconceptions, as evidenced by the remarkable variety of her work. Her writing style was charged with rhetoric, and in describing her tone of voice, contemporaries sometimes come out with a controlled bark. The earlier variations in her surname were probably the result of carelessness, if her correspondence is any guide. Misspellings of simple words like Italians, the running together of words, as in 'gotoItaly', a special code for present participles, so that she could avoid writing 'ing', and a marked lack of punctuation and capital letters are all in evidence.[32] Finally, if her decision to use her married name indicates some form of hidden neurosis, then the implications for married women, in general, are very grim indeed. Her restless spirit seems to have embraced the opportunity for change, a characteristic that gives great vitality to her work. Whatever the reasons, it was during this second visit to Europe that Rose MacPherson became Margaret MacPherson, the new name accompanying changes in style, in her continuing search for forms that would satisfy her imagination.

In addition to her own explorations, Margaret had been busy with a commission from the Board of Trustees of the National Gallery of South Australia to act as adviser and purchaser for the gallery. In this capacity she selected Sir William Orpen's Sowing the Seed[33] – a choice that caused a furore back in Adelaide. In the painting, two small children stand at the edge of a pool, their immature genitalia exposed to public view. Worse still, to their right stands the figure of Nature with her mature genitalia also exposed to view, while she bounteously distributes seed. The Freudian connotations were too much for the worthy citizens of Adelaide and the `local newspapers screamed their fury at the insult offered ... by the deliberately wanton parade of obscenity.'[34] Outraged citizenry scribbled graffiti across the painting, which was hastily but imperfectly expunged before being returned to Orpen. Despite the scandal, Preston continued with the job and in 1915 bought Brangwyn's Bridge at Avignon, a far less contentious decision. The incident must surely have contributed to her 1923 comment in `Why I became a Convert to Modern Art':

> Australia is a fine place in which to think.
>
> The galleries are so well fenced in.
>
> The theatres and cinemas are so well fenced in.
>
> The libraries are so well fenced in.

You do not get bothered with foolish new ideas. Tradition thinks for you...

In 1914 she was busy exhibiting and teaching when, as she put it, `crash, down came the war'.[35] In England she extended her skills by learning pottery, apparently `to try and help mend soldiers'. Her lively intellect thrived on variety and she used craft, at many different times in her life, to relax and refresh herself for her more serious painting and experiment. She wrote an article on pottery in 1930 for Art in Australia, commenting: 'As a profession for women it is a wonder more do not take it up.'[36]

Roger Fry's Omega Workshops (decorative arts workshops) were functioning in London all through the war. Fry believed that the decorative arts could train the eye to appreciate colour and form, a concept echoed by Preston in 'Aboriginal Art Artfully Applied',[37] which she wrote in 1924, using a Roger Fry Omega design to illustrate one of her points. Fry thought that the artist should transform experience into 'a significant grouping of mass and colour',[38] making the design of a picture the channel of communication for the artist's vision. He felt that the graphic arts were an expression of the imaginative life rather than a copy of actual life, a belief that attracted him to children's art because

> children, if left to themselves, never, I believe, copy what they see, never, as we say, 'draw from nature' but express with a delightful freedom and sincerity, the mental images which make up their own imaginative lives.[39]

How close Margaret Preston moved to these ideas can be gathered from her comments in the interview with Woman's Budget in 1931. Speaking of her early paintings she said:

> the difference between my work then and my entirely changed interpretation now is that in those days I copied Nature, as perfectly as possible, setting down every tiny detail just as I saw it. Now I consider that when you have the wonder of Nature framed and hemmed in only by the broad skies and the wide horizons, it is well to look on it and enjoy it as such. Not confine it between four pieces of wood. When we try to imprison that beauty we must make the type of picture fit the frame, and so I design with the utmost care, the exact position of every tiny detail in leaf and flower, bowl or pot which will fit into that frame ... You will find little scraps of paper all over the house when I am designing a new woodcut and woe betide the person who touches one of those scraps.

Again in 1938 in her Carnegie Lectures, she says: 'Art is something made by man to visualise Ideas,' and goes on to quote Clive Bell's 'little girl', who, in answer to the question of how she drew, replied: 'First I think, then I draw a line round my "think".'[40] Fry's emphasis on design as the expression of an artist's mind did not extend to the later structural interpretation of the Bauhaus and neither, do I think, did Preston's, leaving her work free from any association with the sterile functionalism that became a feature of later modernist design.

Her sense of design, like Fry's, was rooted in a sense of order, intelligence and balance, informed by the theories of Cezanne and the Cubists but operating on a more personal, less intellectual level. Her work had far more in common with the modern English painters than it did with the Europeans. Like them, she did lack `not boldness, but a grandeur of conception'.[41]

Rupert Reynell, Gladys's elder brother, was also in England during the war. A Rhodes scholar, Rupert had studied medicine at St Bartholomew's, London after finishing his degree at Oxford, having made the brain his special study. He was one of the pioneers of neurology and when the first victims of shell-shock began arriving back in the country, he was one of the few people who had any idea how to deal with them. It was through him that the two women began to teach pottery and basket-weaving at the Seale-Hayne Neurological Military Hospital, Devonshire, where he was a surgeon.

`She taught the wounded men pottery, to enable them to work with their fingers and help their nerves',[42] William Preston commented over forty years later. Will Dyson, the Australian cartoonist and war artist, expressed his horror at the gulf that separated the Western Front from the English Home Front for, `too many Londoners seemed indifferent.'[43] No such indifference was possible at the Seale-Hayne Hospital, where the two women were daily confronting the effects of battle. Improvisation was the key word due to wartime shortages – an aspect that must have appealed to Margaret's delight in self-sufficiency. In `Pottery as a Profession'[44] she speaks of how `the original mind' can surmount difficulties, and of the ease of building a wood kiln: `no bother, this article being written from actual experience.' Shortages of cane for the basket-weaving were compensated for by young rose shoots, raffia and Paddy's lucerne, `with the result that baskets sold in the town sometimes flowered in the spring.'[45]

Down on the Devon Moors she worked with them until the armistice came and she was free to come home. — 'FROM EGGS TO ELECTROLUX'

Coming home in 1919 via North America, Margaret met second lieutenant William George Preston, thirty-eight years old and recently discharged from the A.I.F. with whom he had served on the Western Front. William Preston was very tall and handsome – a quiet gentlemanly figure. Margaret must have felt immediately in sympathy with the returning Digger, her own experience of war alerting her to what he had been through. Some months after they arrived back in Australia, they were married at Christ Church, O'Halloran Hill, Adelaide, with a wedding reception at Reynella following. Margaret was married from the home of Mrs Carew Reynell, widow of Gladys's eldest brother, who had been killed at Gallipoli. Mrs Lydia Crawford, Gladys's niece, was ten years old at the time and remembers Margaret as 'being great fun. She was staying at our house instead of the big house because my old grandfather Reynell was ill and it was full of nurses.'[46]

Margaret spent some time in Mrs Carew Reynell's house, impressing the young Lydia with her 'frizzy red hair' and a strongly patterned skirt of large windowpane squares – saxe blue with dark grey and white stripes in between. 'It was very unusual', Mrs Crawford commented, 'and I used to think how very attractive it was.' Margaret entertained Lydia and her brother, Richard, by teaching them to draw. She would arrange some fruit on plates or table and observe their childish efforts. 'You see on that side where the light strikes that it is much lighter than on this side where it is in shadow', she would instruct. 'Now, when you're using a pencil you press more firmly on the side where the shadow is and that is how you get a three-dimensional effect.' Also, she got them to pick flowers from the garden and make a pattern with petals and leaves inside the old wooden frames that held glass plate negatives, giving them ideas on how to balance colour and shape. This pattern would then be pressed flat with the glass when the frame was put together again.

'She had very colourful language for the time', Mrs Crawford commented. 'My mother's eyebrows used to shoot up when Margaret used the word "Bloody".' In return for Mrs Carew Reynell's kindness to her, Margaret gave her a still-life, which had been exhibited at the Paris Salon and which depicted bright red geraniums and mauve primulas in a little Chinese porcelain bowl.[47] Mrs Crawford also remembers `the most enchanting Christmas cards' that Margaret used to send them – woodcuts of the brightly coloured lights of the city, seen from across the harbour, and other subjects. For Lydia Reynell's own marriage Preston sent her a woodcut of sunflowers.

When Margaret Preston married, she gave her age as thirty-six, an `error' that was not discovered until some years after her death and that has subsequently lent an air of mystery to her personality. Perhaps there are sinister implications to this lie and evidence of deep trauma and maladjustment. Perhaps, however, there is something entirely understandable about a maiden lady of forty-four, embarking on her first serious relationship with a man, six years her junior, lying about her age. Hal Missingham, in discussing the disparity between her self-portrait (depicting a relatively young woman) and her actual age at the time of painting it (fifty-four) commented: `in all the photographs published none give an indication of her age. (It is a sweet, feminine and touching conceit...)'[48] Her friend, the painter Dorothy Dundas,[49] who knew her from 1929, adds: `She was very feminine in an old fashioned way. She didn't look her age and she always refused to be photographed.' In later years, whenever a photograph or something was needed, Preston would supply either her self-portrait or a photograph that had been taken many years before. Dorothy Dundas commented:

> Age was not something that people gave away in those days. People would never say `Oh, that's too flattering – she doesn't look like that!' They would say `How awful!' if the person was not made to look attractive. It was a prevailing attitude.

Marriage released Preston from the need to earn her living and gave her the advantages, principally extensive travel, that a very good income allows. The couple moved to Musgrave Street, Mosman in 1920 and apart from several years spent at Berowra in the 1930s, lived in various parts of Mosman for the rest of their lives. `When I married I decided to give up teaching and devote myself to this new form of design in still-life,'[50] she said in 1931.

I determined to use my married name and so became Margaret Preston. If my work would not stand, apart from the merit gained under my previous name as an artist, it would have to go. I did not want to be an artist with a name for past merits.

William George Preston was a successful businessman, a company director of the retail chain Anthony Hordern's, Dalton's packaging company and later, Toohey's brewery. He was born in Ryde on 25 August 1881, to George, labourer, and Eliza Preston (née Nicholls). Both parents were English and on the birth certificate, two other children are listed – a brother and a sister. William Preston's decision to settle in Sydney with his new wife was undoubtedly for professional reasons but it was an important decision in terms of Margaret's career, for post-war Sydney was a ferment of artistic activity. A great deal of this activity centred around the Smith & Julius Studios at 24 Bond Street, Sydney, the offices of Sydney Ure Smith, president of the Society of Artists and editor/publisher of Art in Australia. Ure Smith's dual role was of vital importance to Australian art between the wars and extended to the public at large through his other publications – The Home and Australia National Journal.

Margaret Preston came to be intimately associated with these publications, in which, during the 1920s `more space was devoted to articles by, or about, Margaret Preston than any other artist.'[51] In all she wrote fourteen articles for Art in Australia, thirteen for The Home, nine for Australia National Journal and four articles for the Society of Artists yearbooks. As well, three of Ure Smith's major publications were exclusively devoted to her work: the Margaret Preston Number of Art in Australia (1927), Margaret Preston's Recent Paintings (1929), and Margaret Preston's Monotypes (1949).

It is arguable that her current popularity is due not solely to the high quality of her work but also to her approach to her career. Dorothy Dundas said:

She was very productive and she always saw that her work was promoted in a way that was not usual then, but which is taken for granted now. She was very alive to the importance of promotion and used her very strong personality to see that her articles appeared and that her illustrations appeared. She was constantly before the public eye.

In this respect her approach was tailor-made for the present generation, which expects a large serving of theory to accompany the visual arts. On a more practical level it also provides researchers with plenty of material about which to theorize, whereas in the case of an artist like Grace Cossington Smith (of equal importance to Preston in many ways), there is virtually nothing. As Dorothy Dundas said:

> She liked to feel in touch with people and that was tied up with her very direct expression of how she was feeling. Everybody had to know. And she did succeed in presenting herself in a way that she's on record. She's going to be heard.

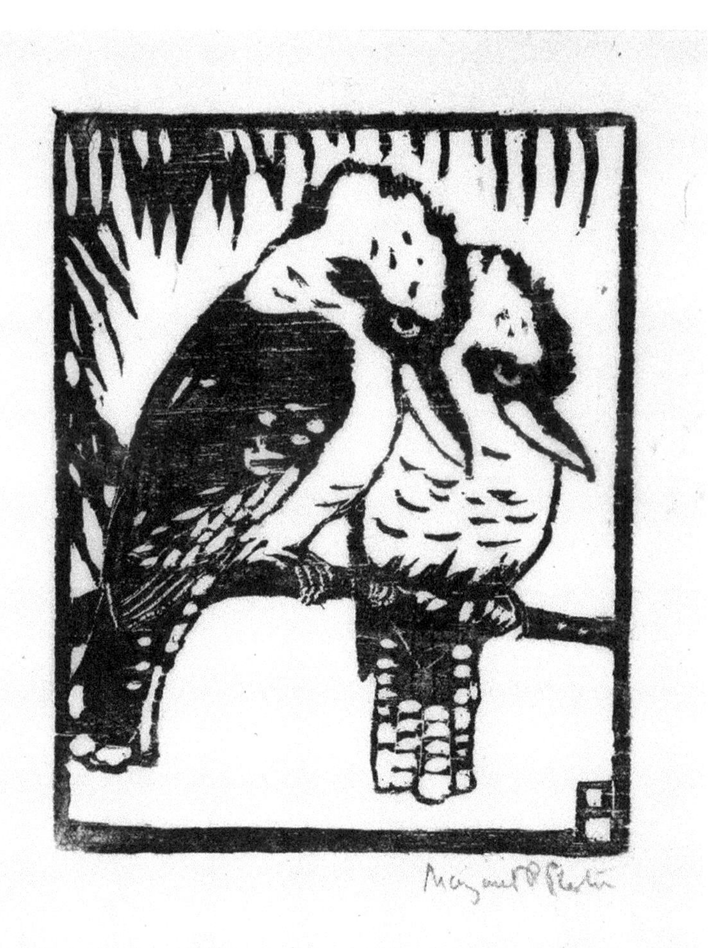

1920–1930

Decoration without ornamentation   Enough or too much
— APHORISM 74

The breadth of enthusiasm and commitment to excellence in publishing that Sydney Ure Smith brought to his involvement with the art world of the 1920s and 1930s created a minor artistic revolution in the city that shared his name. The quarterly journal, Art in Australia, during his period as editor/publisher (1916-39), became, as the venerable Australian artist Lloyd Rees puts it `the first challenge to the supremacy of Melbourne in matters artistic and in other directions as well.'[1] The Melbourne National Gallery School had led the field in academic art training. The Heidelberg School of painters – Tom Roberts, Arthur Streeton, Charles Conder and Fred McCubbin – had established the direction of Australian landscape painting for the twentieth century. Max Meldrum, `the mad Mullah',[2] had claimed a messianic devotion from a generation of Australian artists. Artistic development in Melbourne had been expressed largely through schools of thought and groups of artists, while Sydney, it seems, was always a city of individuals. Ure Smith's election to the presidency of the Society of Artists, which ran parallel to his role as editor/publisher of Art in Australia, increased the scope and influence of the Society, with the prestigious journal acting as a window for its prominent members. On the popular level, Ure Smith's journal of avant-grade good taste, The Home, extended the audience of selected artists to those Australians who were as interested in fashion and interior decoration as they were in fine art.

An advertisement for The Home, in the Melbourne Special Number of Art in Australia, in 1928, headed 'Modernism has reached Australia' stated:

> The wave of modernism which has flooded the intellectual centres of civilised countries has penetrated Australia. It is already perceptible in its art, its music, its architecture, its household furniture and decoration, its literature, its photography and its landscape gardening.

Detailing the mood of 'lighthearted aestheticism' that pervades The Home, the advertisement continues: 'Subscribe now and keep your mind in the mood of the moment and make your home a fit setting for the interesting and brilliant life of this century.'

'After the war, there was an amazing spirit abroad in Sydney' writes Lloyd Rees in his autobiography. 'A triumphant feeling. There was an uprising of intense Australianism which was not confined to the painters but spread to the writers as well.'[3] According to Rees, paganism was rampant, with Norman Lindsay and poet Hugh McCrae peopling the harbour foreshores with Greek gods and goddesses. A number of Sydney artists conducted nude life classes in the sandy coves of the harbour and the area between Martin Place and Circular Quay vibrated with artistic activity. Sydney's fabled hedonism and cosmopolitan affectations had already taken root, allowing 'modern' art to steer a more elegant and superficial course in Tinseltown than in the grey St Petersburg of the south. Alienation, hostility and rebellion against the social order – recurrent tendencies in modernism throughout the twentieth century – found no stronghold in Sydney's artistic circles. By contrast, many of the Melbourne modernists, particularly the younger painters of the 1940s –

Sidney Nolan, Albert Tucker and Arthur Boyd – embraced these attitudes as a central part of their aesthetic.

The modern painters in Sydney did form a loosely knit alliance called the Contemporary Group, in 1926. In it George Washington Lambert, 'the Boldini of Point Piper and Toorak',[4] cast his munificent mantle over the younger modernists with the help of his favourite protégée, Thea Proctor. Lambert's reputation at the time had reached a dizzy height and he was 'disgusted with the lack of appreciation'[5] shown to many of the younger painters, so used his influence to secure a better reception for them. Founding members of the Contemporary Group included Roland Wakelin, Roy de Maistre, Grace Cossington Smith, Adelaide Perry, John D. Moore, Kenneth Macqueen, Elioth Gruner and Margaret Preston. But as Mary Eagle points out, much of their work had a modern look simply because it was unfamiliar. Lambert's pursuit of form for its own sake, Thea Proctor's geometric linear patterning, John D. Moore's formalized studies of Sydney and its environs and the semi-abstract landscapes of Kenneth Macqueen do not, ultimately, amount to a strong engagement with modernism. The claims of other members of the group to such an engagement are better founded, the Wakelin, de Maistre and Cossington Smith trio being long credited with pioneering Post-Impressionism in Australia.

The debate about modernism raged around the predictable scapegoat of moral corruption, Australian society embodying contradictions in the 1920s that were proving difficult to reconcile. For the establishment, evil forces were abroad, threatening to overrun cherished fantasies of Antipodean purity. The fighting spirit of the A.I.F., in peacetime, took on sinister overtones, as did its record of the highest incidence of venereal disease of all the Allied Forces. War profiteers struggled to keep a firm hold on their increasing affluence, while male and female roles continued the process of realignment started by the war. Between 1924 and 1929 more women than men were entering the workforce, taking advantage of their wartime liberation from the invidious practice of job classification. It was finally respectable for single women to earn a living and there was a need for many married women to remain in the workforce to cope with the expansion of the newly mechanized business world.

A paradox existed while the world of business tried to deal with these tensions, exemplified in part at the big Sydney retail stores such as David Jones, Farmers, Grace Brothers and Anthony Horderns. All of these department stores had art galleries, usually on the top floor, promoting in the main, traditional Australian art, which fostered equally traditional Australian values. On the lower floors of the store a different ethic operated, as the retailers cashed in on the vogue for furniture, appliances, clothing and interior decor that was in step with the modern lifestyle. This led to a situation where, as William Moore put it in 1934, `the average girl is quite appreciative of Picasso when seen in a dress material . . .[but] if confronted with a Picasso picture, she would have a fit of laughter.'[6]

The women's magazines of the 1920s were doing their bit to maintain this paradox. They were manuals of economic and efficient behaviour and purveyors of advertising that would determine how and where money should be spent. In addition, they fostered the idea that women need not necessarily regard marriage as a full-time and totally demanding occupation and promoted the arrival of modern technology which lightened the burden of housework.

The Sydney modernists were thus working in a somewhat schizophrenic atmosphere, where their work was much in demand in the commercial sphere but consistently reviled in the creative. The confusion ensuing from so many double-standards undermined the clarity of purpose of many. Their closed ranks against philistine conservatism concealed deep divisions, both of purpose and of practice and blurred the direction of much of their later activity.

Cyril Ritchard's comments upon opening the Contemporary Group show of October 1933 were intended as an admonition to the trustees of the Art Gallery of New South Wales for their lack of interest, but speak to us now of the embattled timidity of many of the group's members.

> I would not call this exhibition a revolutionary one though it is certainly in the new movement. I have seen exhibitions in Paris that are overpowering and frightening, and

which have made me feel that the organisers should provide a handrail for visitors to cling to for moral support.[7]

No handrails were required for the viewing of the Contemporary Group. Their diverse aesthetic concerns were united by their opposition to the prevailing nationalist landscape tradition and their support for contemporary European art, fragmentary though their understanding of that might have been. Margaret Preston was a prominent member of this group but managed to avoid many of the contradictions that dogged others through a combination of circumstance and personality. Her early European training and first-hand experience of Post-Impressionism were allied to a fierce independence of spirit. She was regularly featured in the women's magazines that advocated the new technology as liberation from kitchen-sink reality but her investigations were not compromised by this double-standard. In her own marriage she was not expected to uphold traditional values. She used these publications, just as she did those of Sydney Ure Smith, to air her theories on modern art and its application to the Australian situation, advocating a truly indigenous national art.

Too much craft in art ruins the art in craft — APHORISM 46

One aspect of her art was proving perfectly adapted to the world of graphic illustration – her woodcuts. She found woodblocking `a comfortable kind of craft',[8] working with a vigour that marked her as a woodcutter rather than a wood engraver, and often applying colour by hand after printing. When she wanted to learn more about how to prepare her paper and do the cutting for woodcuts, `she and her husband took a trip to Kyoto in Japan. She studied the technique of woodcutting from the son of the great artist Hiroshige (with a translator),'[9] she informed the Christian Science Monitor in 1954.

The Truth review of the Royal Art Society's exhibition for spring of 1920 referred to her colour prints as `screeches of colour,'[10] noting also the purchase of two still-life paintings – Summer and Nasturtiums – by the National Art Gallery of New South Wales. The lack of official recognition that beset other members of the Contemporary Group was not a feature of her career. The art critic for the Sun, Howard Ashton (later to coin the name `Mad Maggie' for Preston), referred to her woodcuts of 1925 as `bold and slapdash', yet conceded a breadth and courage of design that allowed her `to triumph over far more accomplished engravers'.[11] He also noted her penchant for `unsymmetrical jugs and vases' and his surprise that the woodcuts were so satisfying in spite of such heresy. William Moore, in a review of the same show, referred to her `gorgeously coloured wild flowers'[12] and the combination of balance and rare richness of colour that typified her work. Only the Bulletin, which appeared to be employing a failed stand-up comedian as art critic, struck a negative note, isolating flatness and `far too many colours'[13] as major flaws in the work. Their Adelaide correspondent was more far-sighted, however, when reviewing a show of her woodcuts at the Dunster Gallery the following year. `Many of them may seem to be intentionally crude', he commented, `but the artist is experimenting all along the line, with dainty nudes, views of Sydney Harbour and especially birds and flowers.'[14]

The woodcuts of that year depicting Sydney scenes include Circular Quay, Sydney Heads, Sydney Foreshore, Mosman Bridge, and Wooden Bridge, Mosman. The treatment of these varies, displaying Preston's versatility with the medium. In Circular Quay, block-like forms predominate, with strongly contrasted areas of light and shade giving a monumental weight to the city's quayside. On the other hand, the design of Sydney Heads seems laced together by its tracery of inky black branches and water reflections, the overall feeling of weightlessness aided by the white slivers of sails that are disposed across the centre of the woodcut. Mosman Bridge, built up of a mosaic of clear, bright colour with a daring use of negative space, creates intriguing ambiguities of perspective. The delicate calligraphy which describes the bridge and the expressive, undulating curves of the foliage in the foreground, show Preston's unerring sense of design at its best. The critic for the Sun later commented (7 August 1929): `She has two or three landscapes of Mosman which it is certain would stagger the Mayor and aldermen of that suburb.'

Woodcuts were extremely popular in the 1920s, as Nicholas Draffin has pointed out in Australian Woodcuts and Linocuts of the 1920s and 1930s. Hall Thorpe, the Australian-born artist living in London, extolled the `virtues of modern woodcuts for the private home', stressing `their cheerful, bright, decorative qualities as opposed to the gloomy, depressing and reactionary character of nineteenth century high art, known at second hand through inferior reproductions.'[15]

Margaret Preston seems to have been attracted to the medium for its decorative possibilities and for the discipline that it imposed on her designer's mind: `for the woodcut hinders facility and compels the worker to keep forms in his compositions severe.'[16] For this reason, perhaps, contemporary commentators have seen her woodcuts as `a more radical expression of [her] concerns'[17] than her paintings. The debt she owes to her study of Japanese art is nowhere more evident than in her prints, where daringly simplified composition unites with bounded areas of uninflected colour and a sense of the intuitive and irregular disposition of elements. Dorothy Dundas isolated the `spontaneous charm' of Preston's woodcuts as the reason for their popularity, and this factor, combined with their low prices,[18] was undoubtedly important. Preston's seemingly intuitive command of the medium, however, was allied to a very deliberate manipulation of motif. Her increasing use of native Australian fauna and flora as subject matter was very self-conscious. Her treatment of these motifs displayed a Japanese-derived interest in particularizing nature, through the celebration of its individual units. Her choice of them stemmed from the desire to create a series of uniquely Australian images. If the bush ethos represented by Australian landscape painting was considered masculine in gender, then Margaret Preston's images, spotlighting the detail and variety of bush life, are unquestionably feminine, designed with an uncompromising strength that rids the term of any connotations of sweetness. `No one else seemed to be using Australian flowers' she told the Sydney Morning Herald (3 September 1950), `but I think they are more interesting and decorative than those of other nations.'

Although an advocate of labour-saving devices in the domestic context, Margaret considered that the mechanical reproduction of the printing press gave insensitive results, preferring to do hand printing herself with a Japanese baren (flat pad). There are woodcuts from every phase of her career but it is the woodcuts of the 1920s that represent her most consistent achievement in the medium. From the bold, asymmetrical patterning of Anemones 1925, where border becomes a dominant element of the design, to the expressive linear eloquence and delicacy of Wheel Flower (c. 1929) and the semi-geometric crispness of Gum Blossom (c. 1928), Preston explored the graphic possibilities of the woodcut, elevating it from traditional illustrative applications.

Art, to fulfil its destiny, requires to be accepted by a nation or race and not by a few only – APHORISM 89

Woman's World used Preston woodcuts of banksia, lorikeets, Sturt Peas, and other bush flowers as covers for a number of their magazines during the mid- to late 1920s. The covers ranged from the stark calligraphy of the banksia to an electric blue and red in the lorikeets motif and a muted gaiety in An Autumn Posy. Anemones 1925 became the cover of volume 8, no. 12. One issue, of April 1929, included an article on how to frame the woodcuts:

> making delightful pictures from Woman's World covers. Coloured woodcuts are having a tremendous vogue nowadays, and they make by far the most charming pictures for the very simple or very small room. They give that touch of colour that is so attractive and their simplicity and straightforwardness give them just that decorative asset we need for our walls. Do not waste your covers. They are by the well-known artist, Margaret Preston, and make delightful pictures when framed.

Preston enjoyed exposure to the public eye and there is nothing to suggest that she would have disapproved of this reduction of her 'modernist' principles to the status of household ornament.

As far back as 1914 she had 'allowed herself full licence in colour – only letting her subjects appear as realistic as her aesthetic feeling allowed.'[19] She developed her theories on colour more fully in an article in Art in Australia in 1924,[20] stressing the importance of colour harmony in avoiding discordant effects. There are notebooks revealing that she conducted experiments on a chromatic scale, in line with the theories of Roland Wakelin and Roy de Maistre. 'Black and white . . . appeal to the intellect', she announced, stressing that in all her colour combinations 'I have never found myself out of harmony with nature.'[21]

Along with her woodcuts, her oil paintings of the 1920s continued her consuming interest in still-life, as a vehicle for `the mind of the artist'. She brought her interest in Australian flora into this realm and produced some sumptuous paintings. They are highly organized works and bear an interesting relation to photographs published in The Home in 1924 that accompanied an article on flower arrangement.[22] In the article, Thea Proctor and Margaret Preston discuss the need for design in the arrangement of flowers, with Preston stressing the expressive power of an arrangement and quoting from a fifteenth-century Japanese book on the subject. `Mix your flowers as you do your guests' she advised with characteristic humour; `use due deference to their edges.' Australian Gum Blossom (1928), Double Hibiscus 1929 and Flannel Flowers etc (c. 1936) all bear a strong relationship to the arrangements in the photographs. Equally fascinating is a glimpse of what seems to be the vases that appear in so many of her paintings – the white jug she painted both here and in England and the glass vase used to such strong, geometric effect in Western Australian Gum Blossom 1928. These similarities suggest that her aesthetic moved beyond the mere expression of arid scientific principles in paint into a wider application of decorative design to everyday life. In the `Gentle Art of Arranging Flowers' she quotes Sekishun, who

> once placed some water plants in a flat receptacle to suggest the vegetation of lakes and marshes, and on a wall above he hung a painting by Soami of wild duck flying in the air.

Despite her stated aim of making still-life serve as a laboratory table, there is a rare intimacy and joy in the small event in works like Gladys Reynell's Pottery 1924, depicting Reynell's characteristic blue tea pot and jug, and Thea Proctor's Tea Party 1924, with its wonderful intersecting patterns – checkered tablecloth, patterned china and striped dish. These works, and others of Preston's still-lifes of the period, have a sense of occasion that relates them to the tea ceremony in Japan – the pleasure of the tea master in the blunt solidity of jar or bowl and the process by which the master recognizes the superbly appropriate vessel for the ceremony.

The first purchaser of Thea Proctor's Tea Party, Arthur Allen, unfortunately did not share these sentiments with regard to some aspects of the painting. Preston wrote to Hal Missingham in the late 1950s telling him `the sad story of "Miss Proctor's Tea Party".'[23] George Lambert informed her, shortly after Allen had bought the picture, that its new owner objected to the spoon and knife in the foreground and had taken it upon himself to paste over the offending articles and do a little art work of his own. `Mr Lambert was intensely annoyed over this', she wrote, and `told him that he was liable to the law.'

The painting also takes on new meaning when one learns that Margaret Preston once threw a plate of cakes at Thea Proctor, because the trustees of the New South Wales gallery favoured Thea's work above Margaret's, in a joint exhibition they held at the Grosvenor Galleries.[24] Preston, about 5'4" (162.5 cm) and fiery, arrived to have afternoon tea with Miss Proctor, who was a willowy creature, reputed to be one of the most beautiful women in Sydney. According to Treania Smith the conversation went something like this:

> `Well, have the trustees been?' inquired Margaret. [The trustees had a habit, at the time, of attending every exhibition at the Grosvenor and Macquarie Galleries.]
>
> `Yes they have,' Miss Proctor replied, one imagines rather nervously.
>
> `Did they buy anything?' continued Margaret.
>
> `Yes . . . they bought one of mine.'
>
> Margaret was holding a box of cakes and, throwing them at the astonished Thea, turned on her heel, saying: `There's your afternoon tea.'

Preston is variously reported as hating Nora Heysen's flower studies, sitting on the diminutive and genteel Grace Cossington Smith, and generally reducing to ashes any hapless opponent. Lionel Lindsay regarded her as `the most envious thing I know, a raging creature who burns her work when it doesn't sell. Hasn't one ounce of gratitude in her carcase.'[25] Even the urbane Sydney Ure Smith, an unqualified supporter of her work, had occasion to remark on her dogmatism,[26] while Lloyd Rees maintains `you could have drawn her mouth with a ruler.'[27] According to Dr Rees, Margaret Preston once informed him: `I never forgive!'

Leon Gellert wrote in 1967 that Margaret `had an immense capacity for taking offence. Loyal admirers and friends who had stuck to her through thick and thin were at various times, suddenly and unaccountably ostracised.'[28] Dorothy Dundas felt that her competitiveness stemmed from her awareness of the need for self-promotion, but there was obviously a personality factor at work as well. Elaine Haxton, who, like Dundas, was over thirty years younger than Margaret, remembers her as being very kind and encouraging before Haxton left for England in 1930.

> Everybody was slightly scared of her. She was a very definite person, very bossy, but I found her very nice indeed. She had a commanding personality. She knew what she wanted and she knew what she wanted you to do.[29]

This `bossiness' apparently extended to her subject matter, as The Home noted in 1924: `Margaret Preston does not subserviate her mind to her objects'[30] it announced. `She makes them do what she tells them to do, and look how she tells them to look.' Treania Smith, long-time director of the Macquarie Galleries met Preston in the mid-1930s, when Treania herself was thirty-three.[31]

> Margaret was a dynamic creature. On the first occasion that I met her, she fired questions at me and Beryl Young, pointing her finger at each of us in turn when she wanted our response. I nearly shot up in the air when it was my turn. I thought I'd better be intelligent about art.

Treania remembers her as `a terrific person. She was like a bomb in a room. Everything sparkled and shook when she was about.'

Clearly, Preston was not an easy person to know and seemed to prefer the company of younger people as the years progressed. Her interest in children, and the very positive response of children to her, is on record. Her quick temper seemed to be reserved for her contemporaries and even the very mild-mannered Lloyd Rees, himself twenty years her junior, once commented: `she was a delightful person . . . in an open way one of the most egotistical artists I ever knew.'[32]

Throughout the 1920s the Prestons travelled, their voyaging including New Caledonia and the New Hebrides in 1923; a trip that took in Bali, Singapore, Bangkok, Saigon, Hong Kong and Manila in 1924; China in 1926 and North Queensland in 1927. `My wife . . . was never cluttered up with detail' William Preston remarked;

> she never painted when she was on tours; she seemed to want to get away entirely from art altogether, and when she came back to it she was all the more prepared to go ahead, probably on some new phase entirely.[33]

This ability to refresh herself is evident in the stylistic progression of her work, which is a logical extension of what had gone before but restates essential concerns with freshness and originality. Her impatience with other people was quite possibly related to her, impatience with herself, a feeling she voices in `From Eggs to Electrolux' in 1927:

> Yet again the old restless feeling is bothering her. She feels that her art does not suit the times, that her mentality has changed and that her work is not following her mind. She feels that this is a mechanical age – a scientific one – highly civilised and unaesthetic. She knows that the time has come to express her surroundings in her work.

In her still-life paintings of 1927 Preston departs from the emotive and sensual use of colour of her earlier work. She uses a much more restricted palette and a more graphic use of black and white, which, as she noted `appeal to the intellect'. Blue, which she felt was peculiar to shadow, also plays a prominent role. Implement Blue; Still-Life (depicting kitchen scales, a flour sifter and other implements); Still-Life (depicting a coffee pot and plates stacked for drying); Banksia, Native Heath and Gum Blossoms (all employing an uncompromising and stark simplicity of composition) were painted in this year. They derive, at much remove, from Cubism, which in its deliberate revolt against the Post-Impressionist expressiveness of Gauguin and Van Gogh rejected the sensuous and decorative appeal of colour. Preston's work, moreover, echoed the cylindrical and curvilinear forms of Léger rather than the cubic and rectilinear forms of Picasso and Braque.

One group of cubists loves structure, such as those who love the definite cubic element in a tree, in a landscape, a human body, in the firmness of its cubic anatomy, and the other line of cubism leads away from reality to spiritual expression; it follows the inner lead of any natural object through a maze of angles and balanced lines; it searches for the inner meaning of natural objects — APHORISM 67

The aim of the Cubists had been to create a new way of seeing, in which conventional perspective was abandoned and different aspects of the same object were simultaneously made visible. This was accomplished through a surface arrangement of planes, lines and shapes which overlapped and interlocked in an attempt to reconcile the paradox of three-dimensional volume on a two-dimensional plane. Preston's approach to these problems probably owed as much to the celebration of modernity and labour-saving gadgets that was displayed in the many magazines of the day as it did to any close engagement with Analytical Cubism. As Ann Stephen points out in Art Network,[34] her images shared the same currency of construction as the commercial photography of the period, which favoured oblique angles of perception and dramatic lighting effects, and stressed the formal or abstract qualities of what was being photographed.

While these still-lifes emphasize a very shallow picture space, reduce elements to radically simplified intersecting planes and use cast shadows as key elements in the composition, they do not challenge our vision of reality in the way that Cubism has. Preston's interest in Cézanne's spheres, cones and cylinders was certainly an attempt to come to terms with underlying structure but it was also her designer's love of simplified shape. Even in this `geometric modern phase'[35] of her work there is no engagement with the more radical fracturing of shape and dynamic presentation of multi-faceted reality that took place with Picasso, Braque and Léger. Her interest in the linear, symbolic abstraction of Aboriginal art (see section 1924-63) does relate to some of the issues of Synthetic Cubism, however, in its attempt to create a reality that parallels our own with a language of visual signs.

There were some fundamental limitations in the interpretation of Cubism that Preston expressed in her writings and lectures. In the Carnegie Lectures of 1938 she states that it was Cézanne who said that nature could be expressed by the cube, the cone and the cylinder. Cézanne did not mention the cube in his famous statement to Emile Bernard about treating nature `in terms of the sphere, cone and cylinder', and although its inclusion can be assumed, this imprecision on her part is characteristic of her descriptions. For Preston, Cubism's importance lay in its reliance on geometry and its revulsion against photographic realism in technique (Manuscripts, no. 4, 1933). Of Picasso and Braque's aim to present one synthesized view of the knowledge we have of the three-dimensional nature of objects, of the visual statements they made on relativity and connection, there is no coherent discussion. Her interpretation of Cubism in her own work was as a form of schematized design which borrowed mannerisms of style but not intention. Nonetheless, some powerful paintings resulted.

An important painting of 1928 was Western Australian Gum Blossom. In it, Preston employed the dramatically restricted palette of 1927, where black and white are infused with faintly acidic colour, somewhat in the manner of a hand-tinted, black and white photograph. The gum nuts in the painting are solid spheres, the vase a reflective cylinder and the leaves a series of brittle, anxious planes that bend and twist around the central, vertical motif. Stark rectangles of light and dark tones high-light the image, the whole composition expressing a potent force quite out of proportion to the apparent subject matter. The lush harmonies and graceful opulence of the earlier still-life paintings have given way in this image to an uncompromising austerity that contains an explosive tension. Eucalyptus and Aboriginal Flowers, also painted in 1928, share many of the same concerns. That she was still experimenting in this area is evidenced by another very different painting of that year, Australian Gum Blossom. Its arrangement of brightly coloured blossoms forms a richly variegated pattern that exists on a flat plane with the traces of leaf and flower on the wall behind. The oblique viewpoint of the composition makes the table a flat disc that sustains the circular shape of the flower arrangement in a particularly satisfying way.

Daniel Thomas pinpoints 1928-29 as the year when art deco reached its peak in Australia.[36] He also notes that a favourite art deco plant was the cactus (its Australian equivalent being the banksia) because of its solid cylindrical shape and association with the art colonies of New Mexico. Banksia were a favourite subject for Preston and she was attracted by cactus too as is evident from the fine colour plate that accompanies Recent Paintings (1929). She alluded to her use of banksia as subject matter in an article in Art in Australia (3rd Series, no. 59) in 1935:

> My fondness for painting banksia is due to the simplicity of their form and colour. They allow other material in the composition to have an equally dominant position in the scheme, without appearing to do so.

Art deco, a decorative style that stresses simple, massive forms, takes its name from the Exposition Internationale des Arts Décoratifs et Industriels Modernes that took place in Paris in 1925. By the late 1920s the language of Cubism had surfaced in the vocabulary of art deco as a mannerism, and decoration and design took on faceted, angular forms. The fashionable connotations associated with this style would not have escaped Margaret Preston, who must have been looking at the women's and décor magazines, if only to read her own articles and those of her friends. This is not to suggest that her explorations were trivial (popular culture and the minor arts having long been acceptable source material) but simply to appreciate them for what they are, the work of a woman who reacted to her times in an honest, uncompromising way.

Art in Australia devoted a special issue to Margaret Preston in 1927, which included the geometric modern paintings of that year, three of them in colour. The previous issue contained an article on design and noted that `Margaret Preston insisted fiercely on the importance of design and endeavoured to woo us from our persistent preoccupation with naturalism.'[37]

The special issue of December 1927 was an unequivocal salute to her work. The editorial spoke of her `unerring and instinctive knowledge of colour and pattern', her `strength, vitality and ... originality'. She was, it announced, `the natural enemy of the dull'. Thea Proctor rhapsodized over Preston's work in another part of the journal,[38] singling out her `amazing versatility' and `emotional colour sense' for special praise. She spoke of the effects the return to the Australian light had on Preston's colour, gradually making it `richer and more intense, until, after a visit to the Islands, it developed into a positive voluptuousness of sumptuous colour.' Proctor also deplored the lack of recognition accorded to Preston at the time, a sentiment taken up by A. Radcliff Brown in the article `Margaret Preston and Transition' also in the special issue:

> I find it very difficult to see what it is in her work [her critics] object to. There is nothing startling, nothing revolutionary, or nothing that would seem so in Europe or America ... she has gradually developed a style of her own that both expresses her individual vision of the world and also has absorbed something of the modern spirit that is permeating our lives.

He notes the restrained harmony of the later work and comments on the geometric modern paintings.

At first glance these look as if they were painted in black and white ... Only a longer scrutiny reveals that they are full of subdued colour which, by its very restraint, makes a more lasting appeal ... It is, of course, a well known method in Chinese and Japanese art, but Mrs Preston has used it in her own original way.

Their acute awareness of this lack of appreciation may have been more a general lament for the modern painters, because Preston's work was not quite so ignored as their defence of it suggests. The Art Gallery of New South Wales had consistently acquired her work since she moved to Sydney, as evidenced by their splendid collection today. Of eight paintings she submitted to the Society of Artists exhibition in September 1924, six were sold and this was by no means an unusual occurrence. Among her fellow artists, there was `a positive lust for possesion' of her painting as Thea Proctor admits,[39] and reviews of her exhibitions were frequently praiseworthy and sympathetic. By the end of the 1920s she had acquired a wider audience through magazines like Woman's World, The Home and Wentworth Magazine and Treania Smith remembers her as one of the few bestsellers at the Macquarie Galleries. In 1928, the same year as it was painted, Australian Gum Blossom was acquired by the Art Gallery of New South Wales and Art in Australia issued a print of the painting, which sold for 10s 6d. In 1929 Ure Smith published a handsome portfolio of woodcuts and colour prints of her paintings and in the same year she was the first woman artist to be requested by the Art Gallery of New South Wales to paint her self-portrait. Furthermore, she was only the eleventh artist to receive such a request since the gallery came into existence the year before she was born.

By contrast, the work of Grace Cossington Smith sold so badly that, when she was `rediscovered' in the early 1970s, the Macquarie Galleries had virtually all of her work from the previous fifty years to sell.

Preston had experimented with portraiture before she went to Europe for the second time, but had abandoned it in favour of her beloved still-life. In 1950, she told the Sydney Morning Herald: `I gave it up because people used to grumble at the likenesses.'[40] In her maturity, the only person she seems to have found compelling enough to paint was her husband (1925). The gallery's request was irresistible, however, and in April 1930 she told the Sun: `Yes, my self-portrait is completed, but I am a flower painter and I am not a flower.'[41] The self-portrait has been accused of being `mask-like'[42] and yet she has painted herself in full sunlight, her neck rising, like one of her solid cylindrical vases, from the graphic flatness of her black dress. Behind her a brick wall creates an irregular pattern and beside her rests a pot of wild flowers.

`The self-portrait is very like her' Treania Smith commented. `She did not look her age. You get her eyes in it – the intensity of them – as if they're out on sticks.' Hal Missingham saw it as `self-contained' and displaying `great purpose in the firmness of the thumb holding the palette ... a brick-wall background, set as 4-square as her Scottish character.'[43]

During the 1930s, Margaret Preston was, creatively speaking, marking time. She did a lot of travelling in these years, to such places as New Zealand, Peking, Korea and Japan, and throughout the Americas. She moved to the bush for three years, was ill and did quite an amount of lecturing and writing. Her paintings of the period reflect her continued interest in Australian flora but lack the exquisite grace of her 1920s studies and the intriguing originality of her work of the 1940s. Banksia Cobs of 1933 continues her interest in the restrained palette of 1927-28, but without the dynamic compositional elements of those years. A woodcut of about 1936, Australian Rock Lily, is a more successful work and the delicacy of its sprays of star-shaped flowers emerging from their weaving, stylized base, is an elegant continuation of her great achievements in this medium. Rose and Banksia, 1936, has a theatrical quality that is not a common feature of her work. The florid arrangement and rather capricious disposition of elements relates to the vaguely surrealist floral designs of Adrian Feint, an intimate of Preston's who enjoyed wide popularity during this period. This tendency is also present, in a lesser degree, in Banksia, 1938, where fronds of fern and leafy tendrils arch over the solid, slightly garish cylinders of banksia.

Margaret Preston was not so much lost in these years as looking for `even one form that will suggest Australia in some way',[44] a form she was to find through her application of certain principles of Aboriginal art to her personal aesthetic.

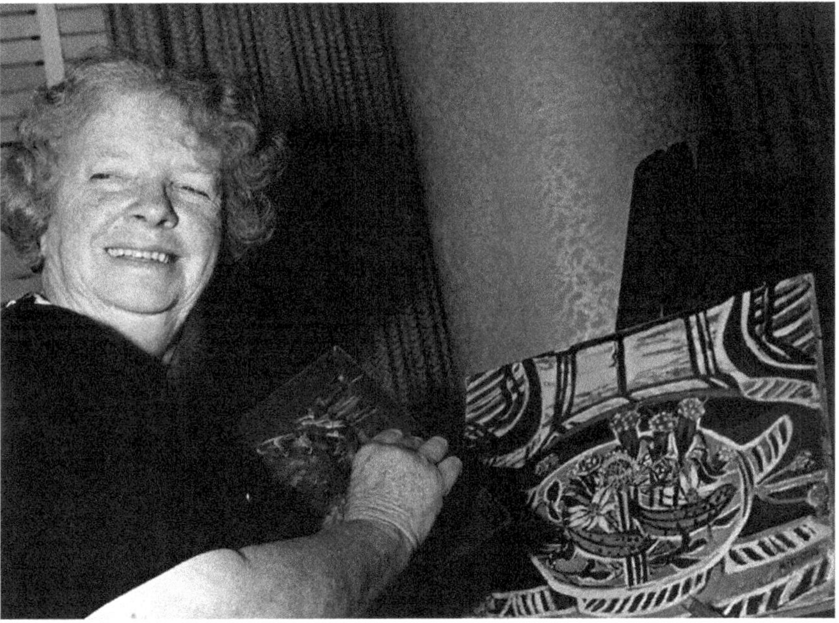

Margaret Preston 1946.

1924–1963

Be Aboriginal[1]

Through the 1920s while Margaret Preston was painting still-life and rescuing Australian flora from 'its customary banal exploitation at the hands of most of our artistic craftsmen',[2] a related passion was gaining momentum – the need to develop a truly indigenous Australian art.

'What creative art have you in Australia?' she asked the Public Questions Society of Sydney University in 1924. 'None whatsoever.'[3] Preston felt that Australian art had atrophied in a series of traditional heroic poses. Each century had the art that was most characteristic of its time, she argued, and if there was no movement in art then the intelligence of the people was at a standstill. By December of that year she had published an article in The Home, 'Aboriginal Art Artfully Applied',[4] which set out some of the ideas that were to preoccupy her in the following decades, culminating in her Aboriginal-inspired style of the 1940s. Her concern centred on the lack of distinctive Australian designs, a void that she felt could not be filled by her own interest in wild flowers. `Taking native flowers etc of any country and twiddling them into unique forms will never give a national decorative art', she wrote. `A study of our own aboriginal art may meet with better success.' With the knowledge that European art had not been above borrowing from `primitive' cultures, she saw the application of Aboriginal art to design as an escape from `the South Kensington dullness which has pervaded and perverted the decorative impulse of this country.'

Within the next few years these observations grew into a fully developed theory, which she would expound on almost every possible occasion, frequently with a marked lack of logic. Her championing of Aboriginal art was accompanied by a virulent artistic colonialism, which advocated the adoption of Aboriginal methods and ways of seeing but at the same time, denied the culture that gave them meaning. There is no question that her theories were rife with racist assumptions but she was, by all accounts, an imperious creature and her crude analysis of `the savage mind'[5] was probably due as much to a brutal directness of character as it was to conventional racist attitudes.

The search for a national cultural identity preoccupied diverse groups of Australians between the wars. The Nationalist Party, presided over by Billy Hughes and later Stanley Melbourne Bruce and Earle Page, declared their principles under Bruce/Page (with no irony intended) as `loyalty to the King, the maintenance of the unity of the British Empire and the continuance of constitutional government.'[6] They ushered in a period of government violently opposed to Bolshevism, which in the arts was believed to be represented by modernism. Australia was still seen by many of the crusading nationalists as a country defined by its physical environment and its tradition of bush pioneers, whose exploits and mythic relationship to the bush provided the source and inspiration for creative endeavour. The fact that Australia, in the 1920s, was already a highly urbanized country was side-stepped by writers like Louis Esson and Vance Palmer, who looked back to the 1890s for an epic quality they could not find in the present. On other fronts, rabid individualists like Norman Lindsay promoted their own eccentric brand of nationalism, based in his case on the idea of an Australian renaissance, a pot-pourri of faery and Greek mythology which rejected internationalism as if it were a contagious disease. At an official level there was endorsement of reactionary artists, gallery directors and art educators, and a lack of opportunity or encouragement for Australian writers and poets.

Preston embraced modernism but violently rejected internationalism (a fact that is, itself, a contradiction). 'Art is not cosmopolitan' she stated in 1925. 'Our saving grace is our distance from contaminating sources.'[7] Despite the fact that she herself had gained so much from travel and European training, she could still say: 'We have teachers and wonderful prints to help us and the rest must come from ourselves', and five years later, in 1930: 'Let us have no travelling for our budding artists!'[8] Perhaps, like Norman Lindsay, she felt that a renaissance was possible in Australia simply because she was here to lead it.

Historically, the older form of Australian nationalism had been identified with the Left, and with right-wing parties dominating politics up to the late 1920s, there was little hope of any official support for nationalist ideals. With the election to office of the Labor Party in 1929, however, followed by the radicalizing effects of the Depression, a new spirit was infused into nationalist theorizing and alongside it a more progressive form of cultural identity. The 1930s saw the formation of groups like the Jindyworobak movement, led by Rex Ingamells, which published poetry incorporating Aboriginal words. Jindyworobak is an Aboriginal word meaning 'to annex, to join', the group sharing some of Margaret Preston's beliefs. Their aim was 'to express something of the Australian place spirit which baffles expression in English words, so often coloured by European associations.'[9] The group is now seen as more important as a meeting place for writers and artists than for the poetry it produced, but it will be no surprise to learn that Margaret Preston respected its aims and, at times, contributed illustrations for Jindyworobak anthologies. Preston was also sympathetic to the Australia First Movement, through her friendship with the poet Ian Mudie, who was a member of the Jindyworobaks.

In 1925, the year in which Margaret Preston really began campaigning for a national art based on Aboriginal art forms, the first Australian chair in anthropology was being established at Sydney University. It was in the years that followed that the writing of people like Professor A. P. Elkin, Frederick D. McCarthy and Charles P. Mountford, started to reach a popular audience and change our perceptions of Aboriginal culture and society. Thus Preston's own explorations were gradually informed by the knowledge that these anthropologists were amassing, as is witnessed by her reference to McCarthy in an article of 1940. This makes the contradictions in her own writings all the more difficult to understand, unless we subscribe to the opinion of one of her contemporaries: 'She would never listen to anyone. That's why she was so good.'[10]

The main thrust of these contradictions was in her attitude to the totemic aspects of Aboriginal art, the mythological and religious symbolism of the Aboriginal people. She seemed to recognize the power of such motivations, saying in 1925: 'totemism is one of the origins of art',[11] and again, in 1941, 'the study of the work of the Australian aborigines is nearly exhaustless. Through its Totemism (inherent vision) it opens up a new world for the Australian artist.'[12] Despite these statements, she was also able to say, in 1930: the student must be careful not to bother about what myths the carver may have tried to illustrate. Mythology and symbolism do not matter to the artist, only to the anthropologist.[13]

And again in 1946:

> The totemic part of their work is another branch of study which does not come into the latitude of plastic art, any more than the religious views of the Van Eycks in their magnificent, aesthetic and cultural art.[14]

Her comparison with the Flemish artists is a good example of Preston's journalese. Over the years she employed a number of eye-catching comparisons (often culinary, although she claimed she was no cook) that make for good copy rather than informed statement. Another example is her equating of the Sydney Harbour Bridge with the 'worship of iron bound realism that has ruled the art of Australia generally', lumping the bridge, Sydney's Archibald Fountain and Martin Place cenotaph into an unholy union as related examples of 'Meccano Art'.[18] Preston would have known from reading McCarthy's book, Australian Aboriginal Decorative Art of 1938, that the art of the Aboriginals 'is more than a mere expres-

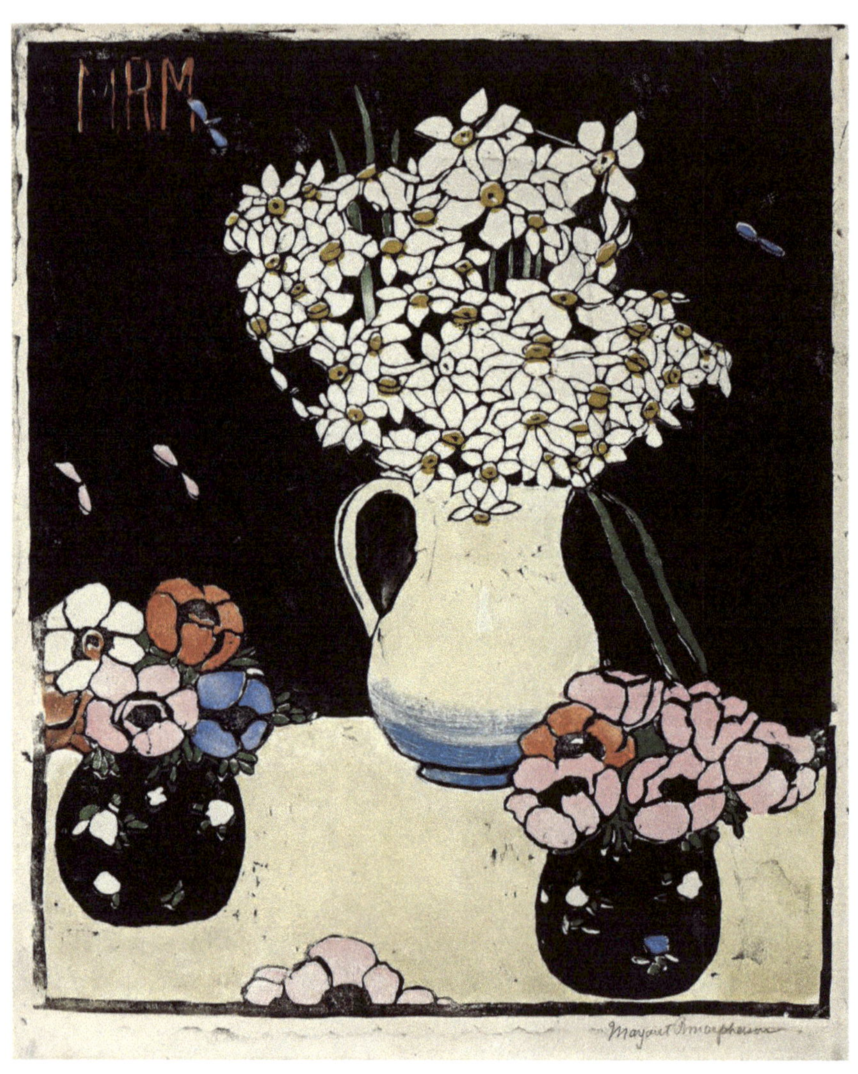

Narcissi, c 1917. Hand-coloured woodcut, signed MRM in plate.

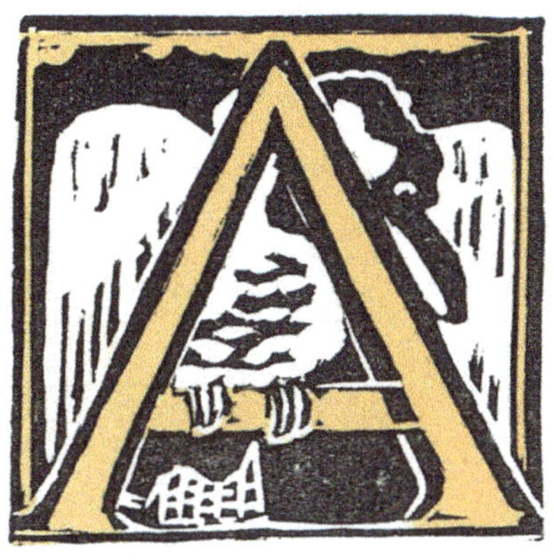
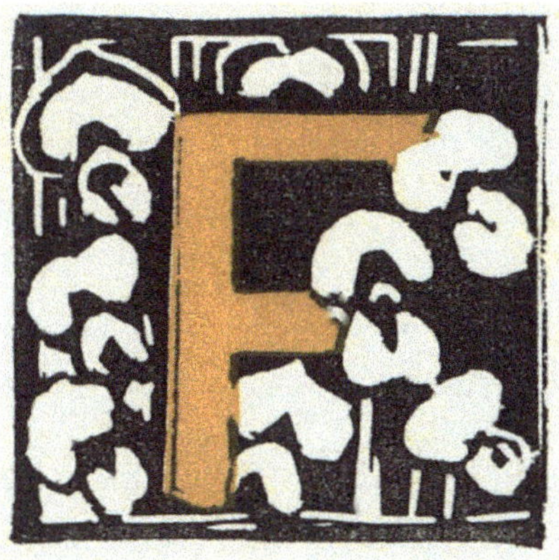
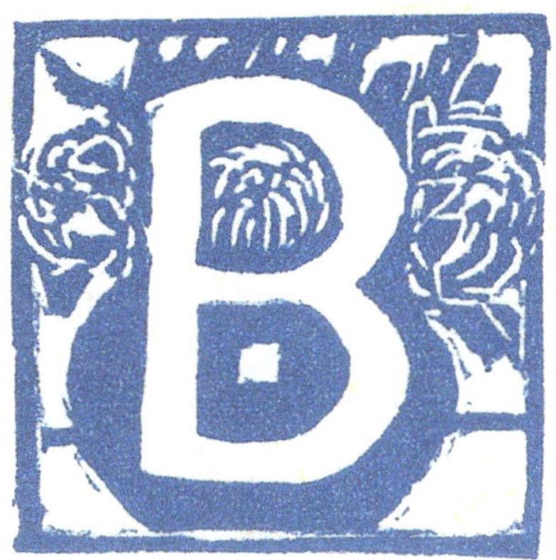
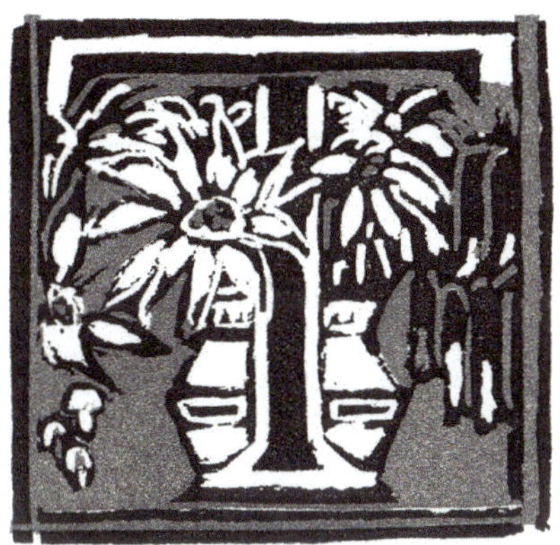
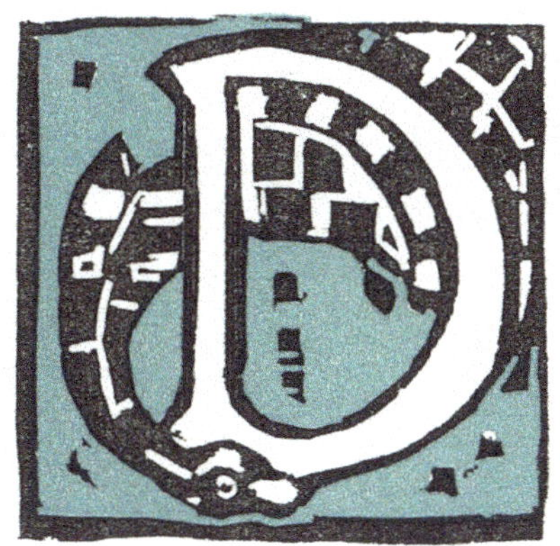
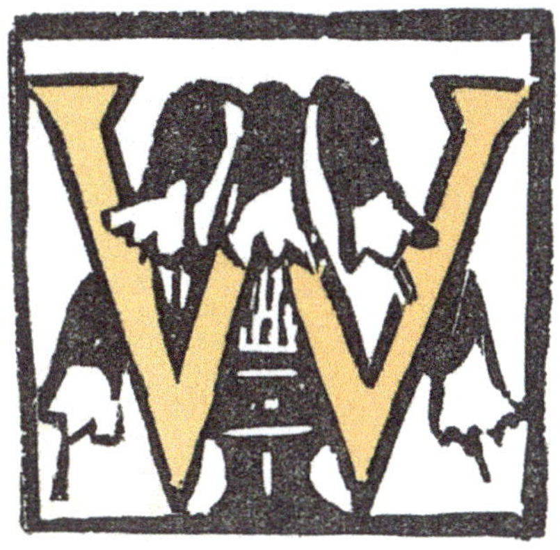

Letters of the Alphabet, as reproduced in Art in Australia 1923-25.

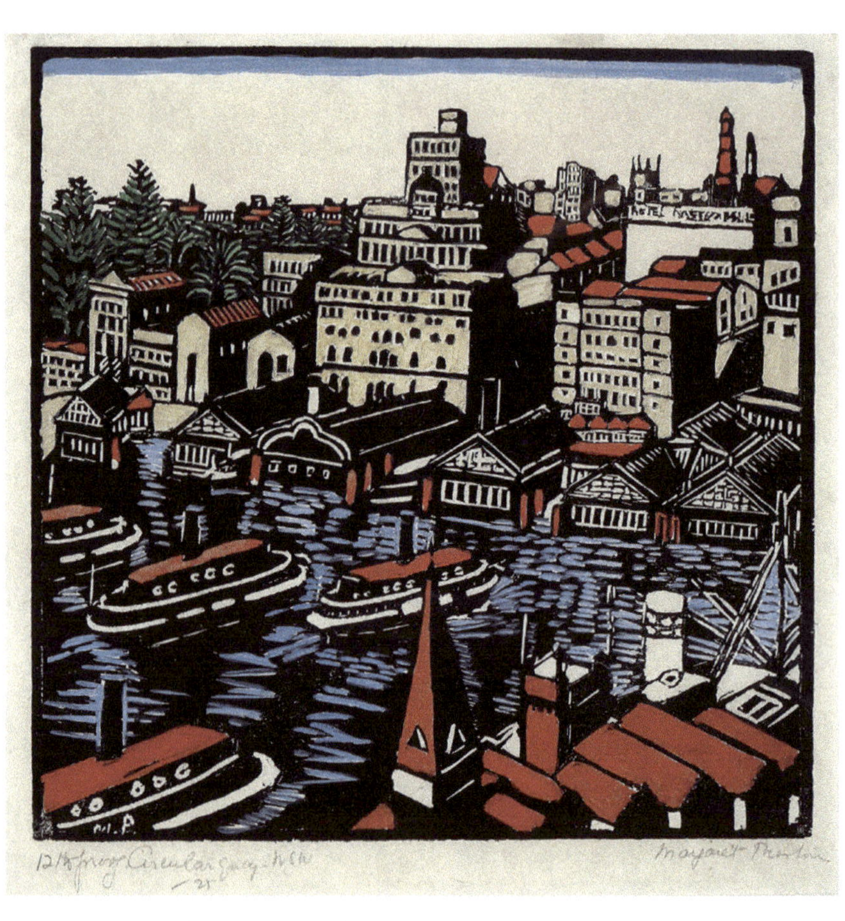

Circular Quay, 12 th Proof. Hand-coloured woodcut 1925.

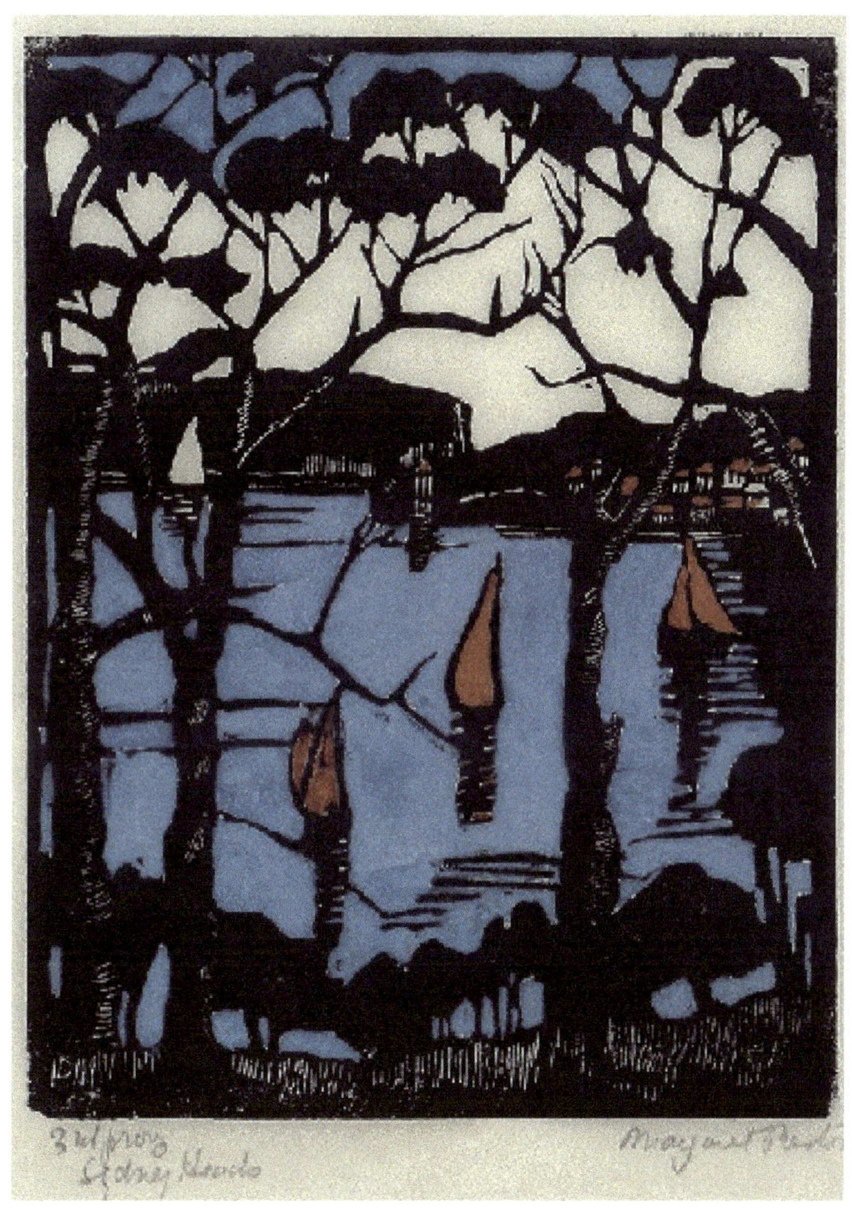

Sydney Heads 1925. Hand-coloured woodcut.

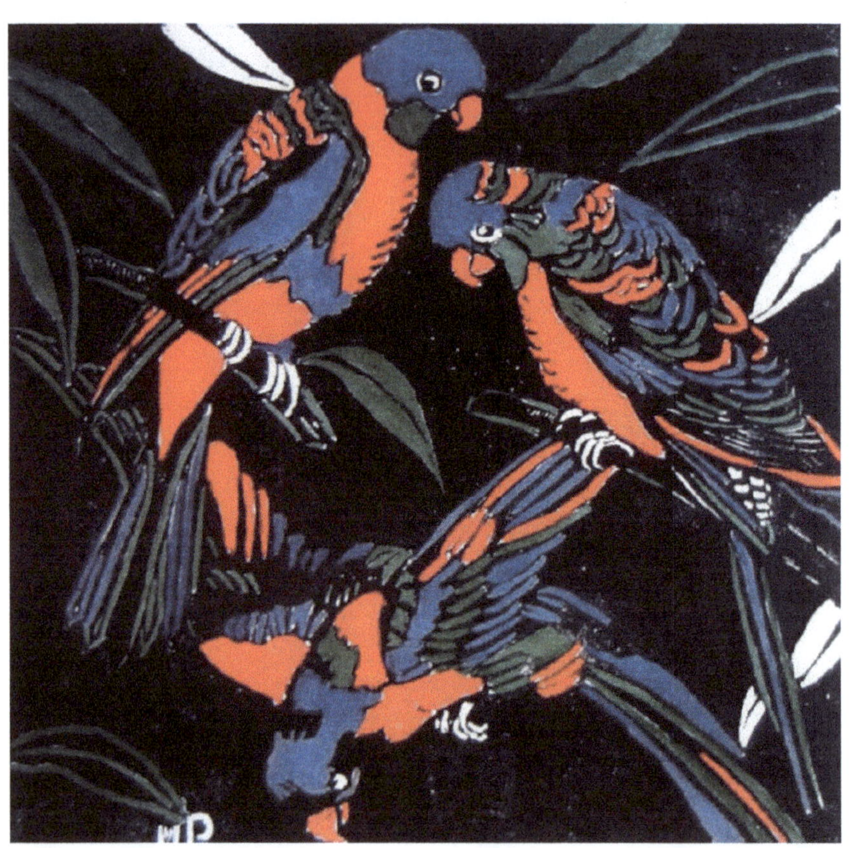

Lorikeets, 1925. Coloured woodblock.

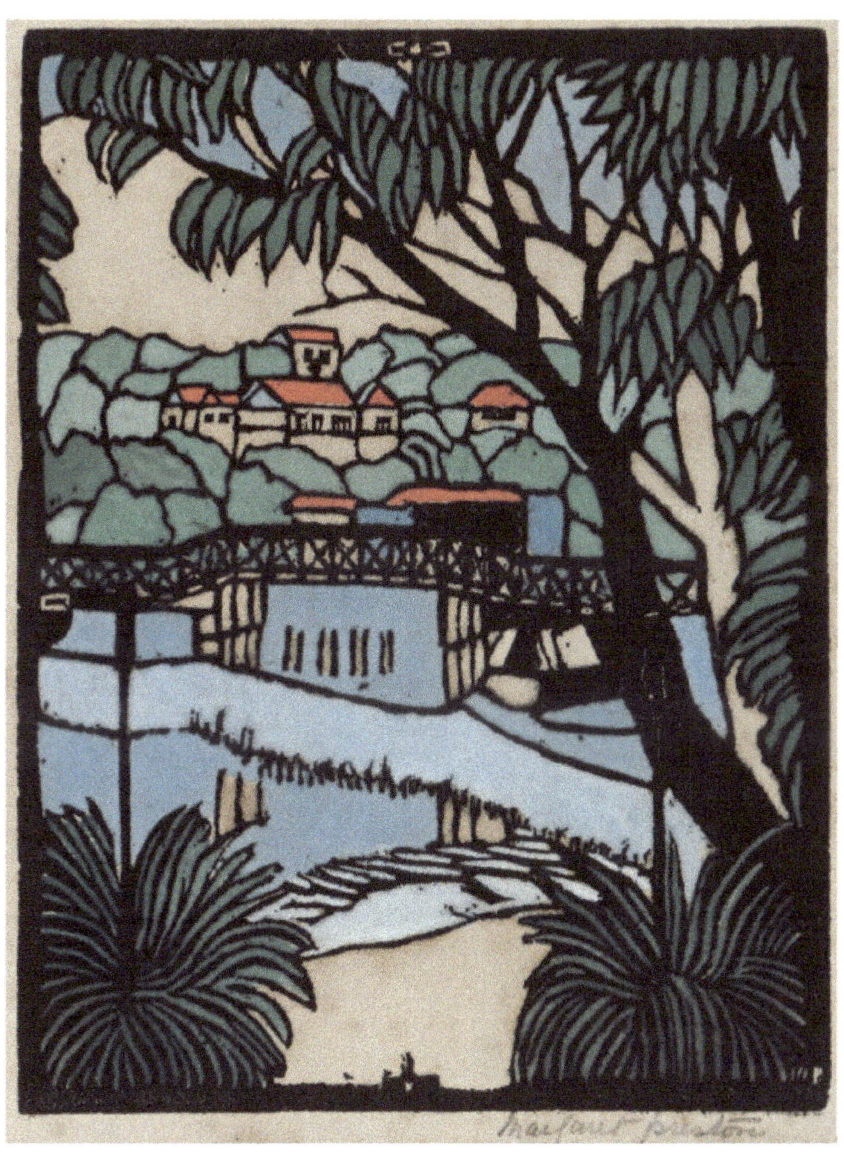

Mosman Bridge, 1927. Hand-coloured woodcut.

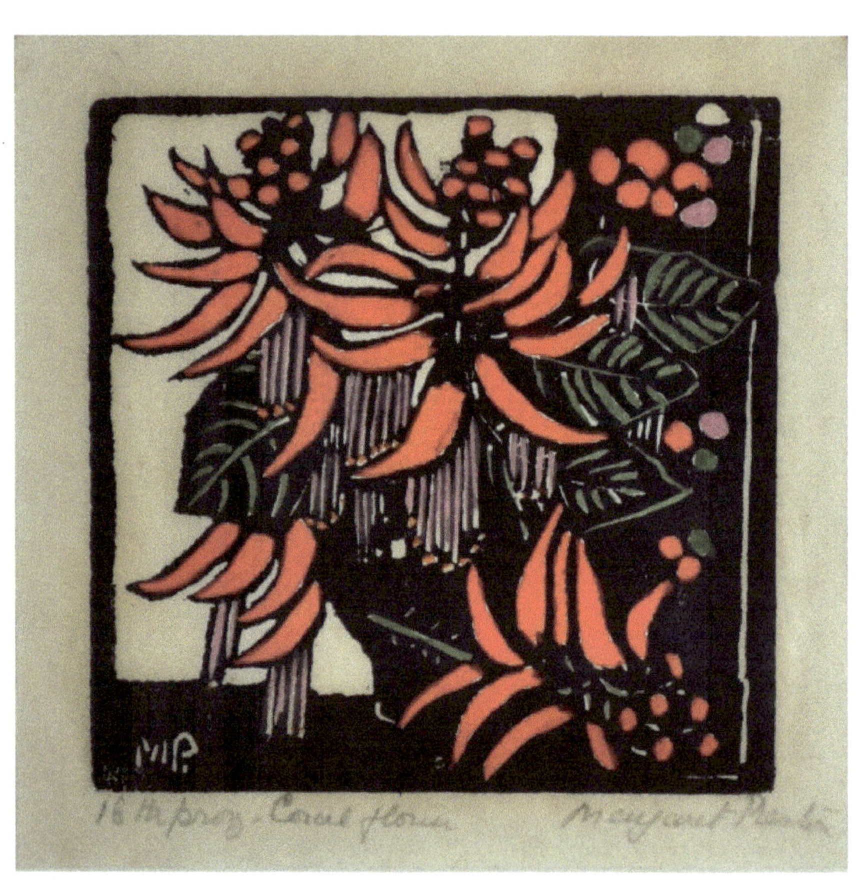

Coral Flower, 1928. Hand-coloured woodcut.

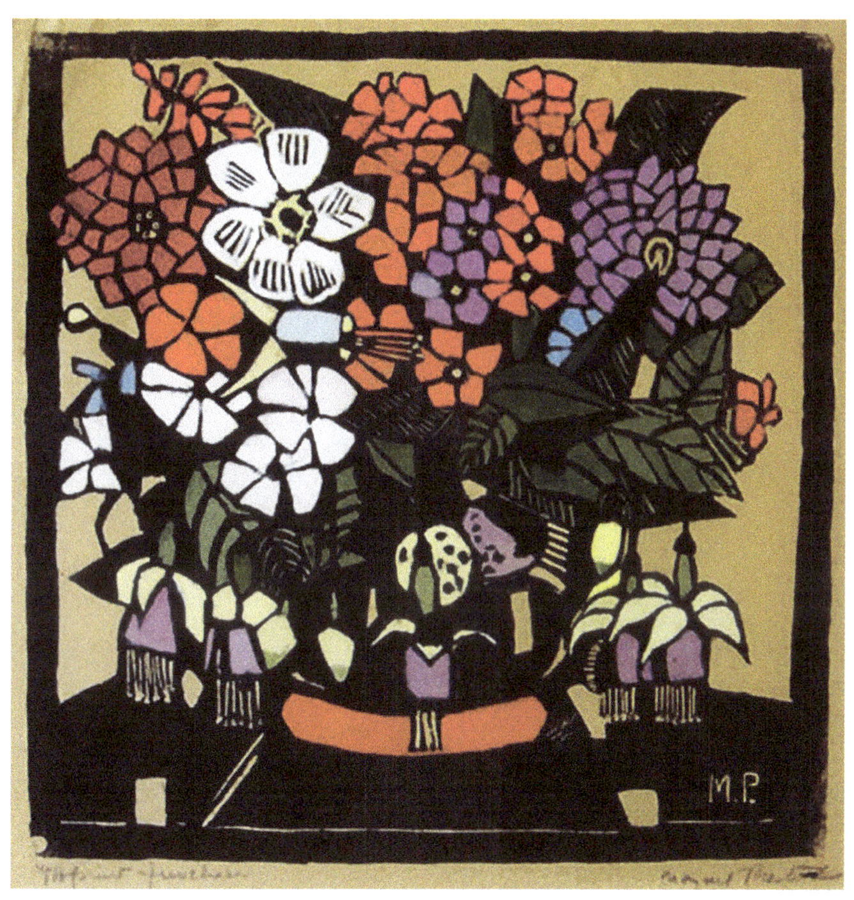

Fushia, 1928.

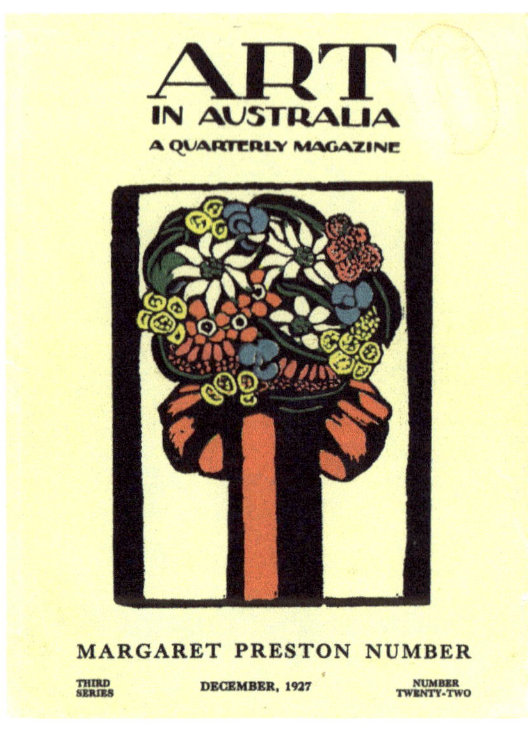
ART
IN AUSTRALIA
A QUARTERLY MAGAZINE
MARGARET PRESTON NUMBER
THIRD SERIES
DECEMBER, 1927
NUMBER TWENTY-TWO

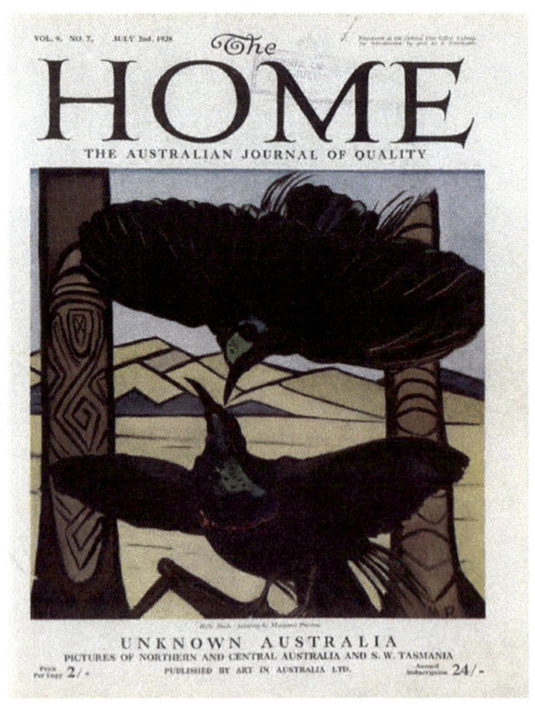
VOL. 9, NO. 7, JULY 2nd, 1928
The
HOME
THE AUSTRALIAN JOURNAL OF QUALITY
UNKNOWN AUSTRALIA
PICTURES OF NORTHERN AND CENTRAL AUSTRALIA AND S. W. TASMANIA
Price Per Copy 2/-
PUBLISHED BY ART IN AUSTRALIA LTD.
Annual Subscription 24/-

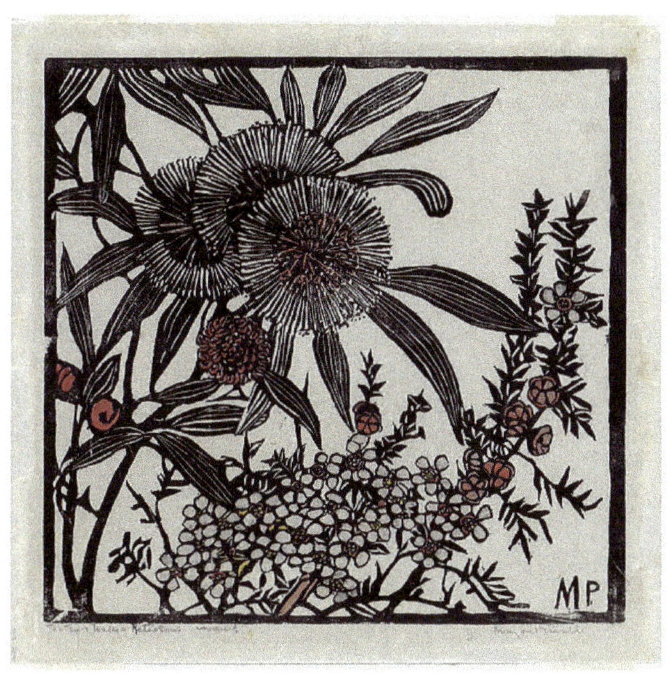

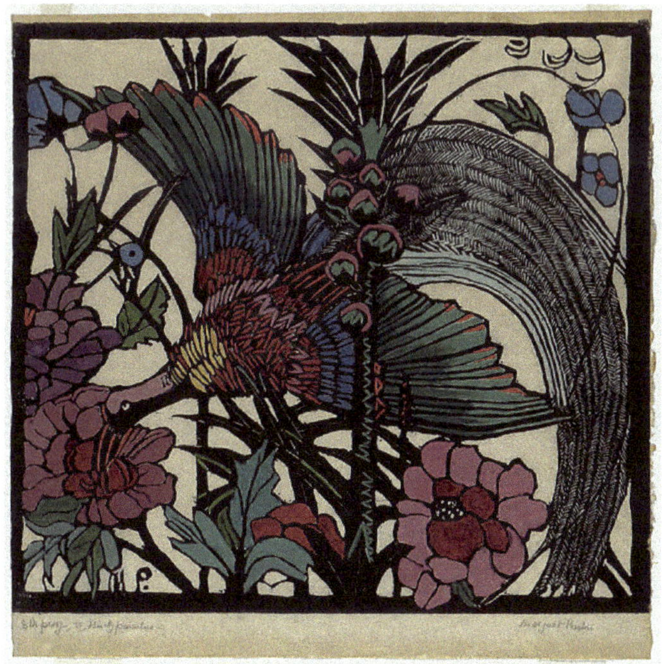

Bird of Paradise & Tea-Tree and Hakia. Hand-coloured woodcuts.

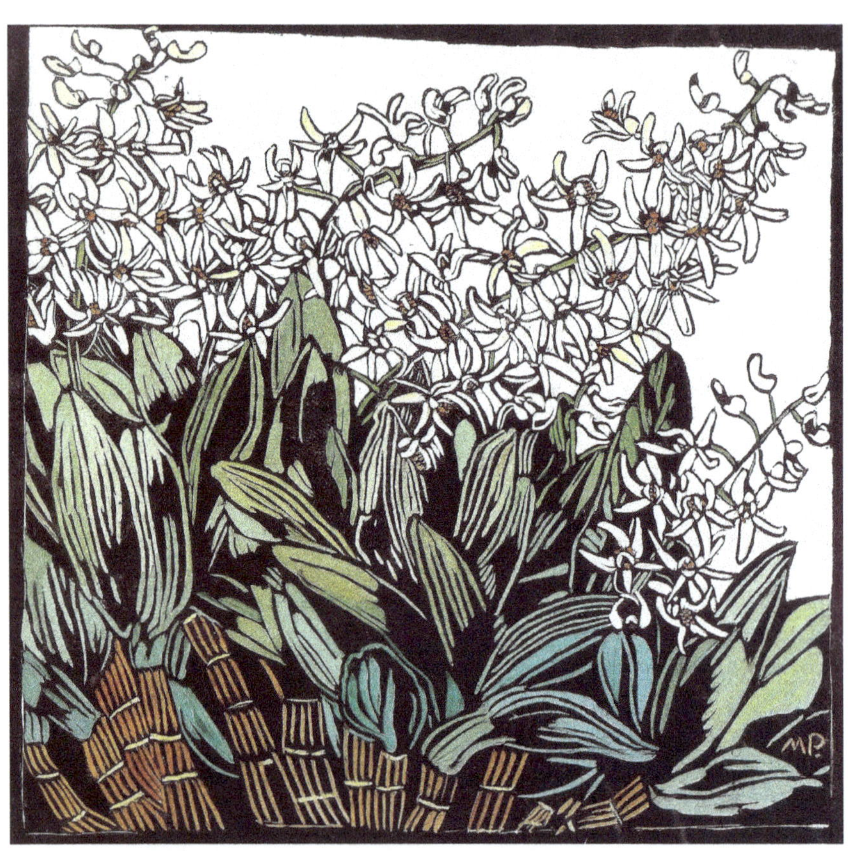

Rock Lilly, 1936. Hand-coloured woodcut.

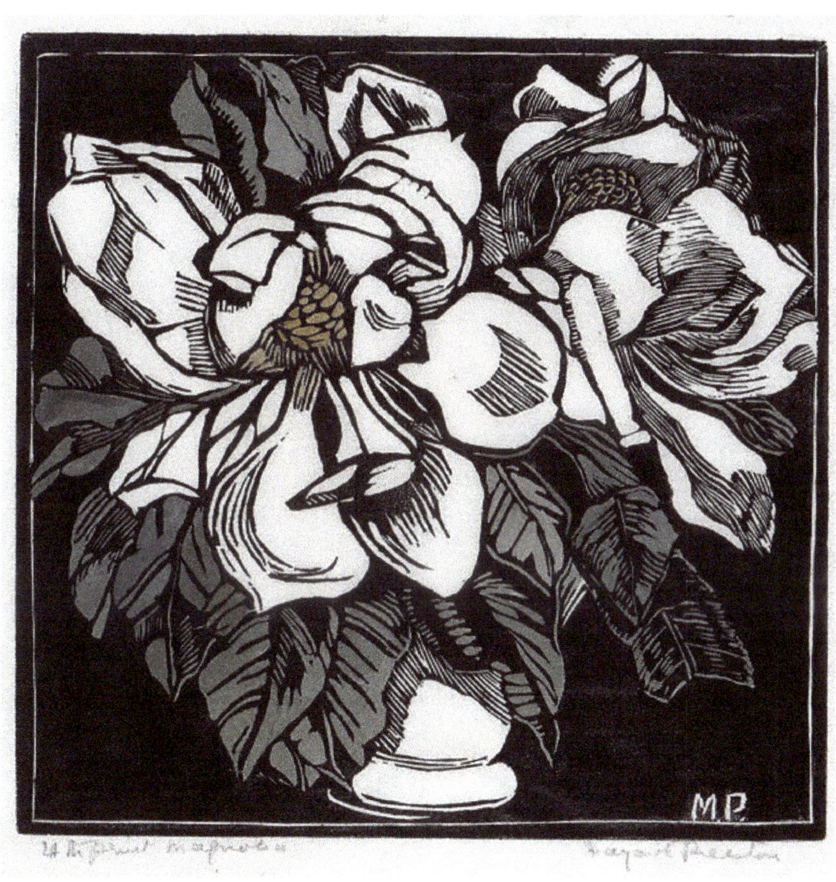

Magnolia, 1937. Hand-coloured woodcut.

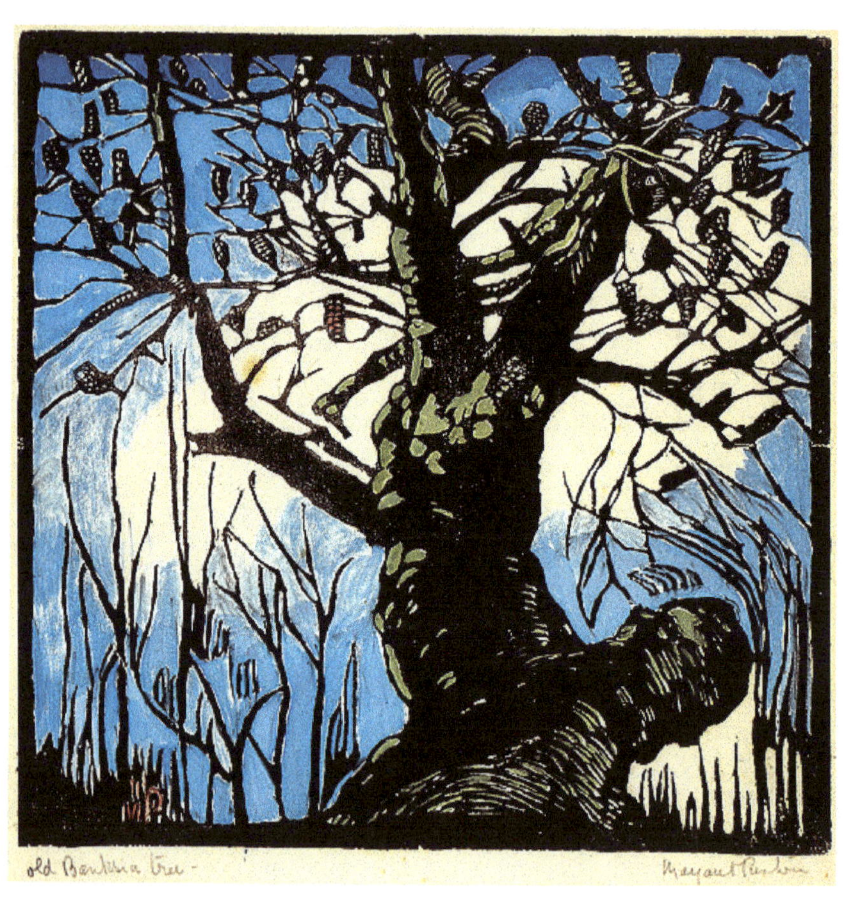

Banksia Tree, 1939. Hand-coloured woodcut.

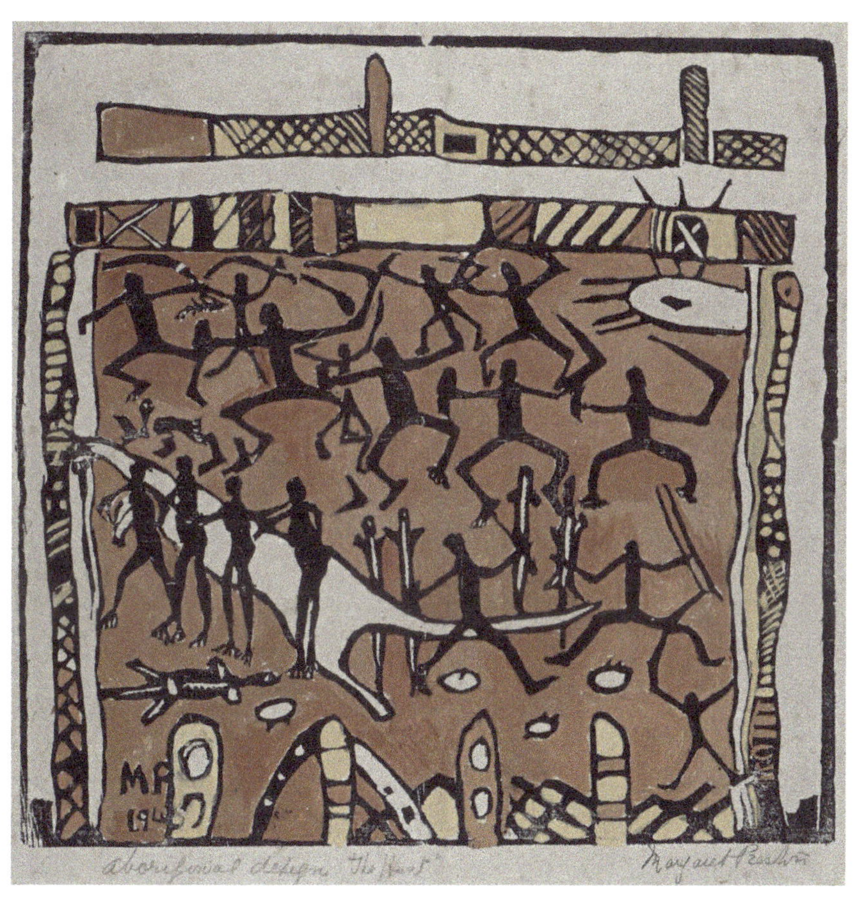

Aboriginal Design, 1940. Hand-coloured woodcut.

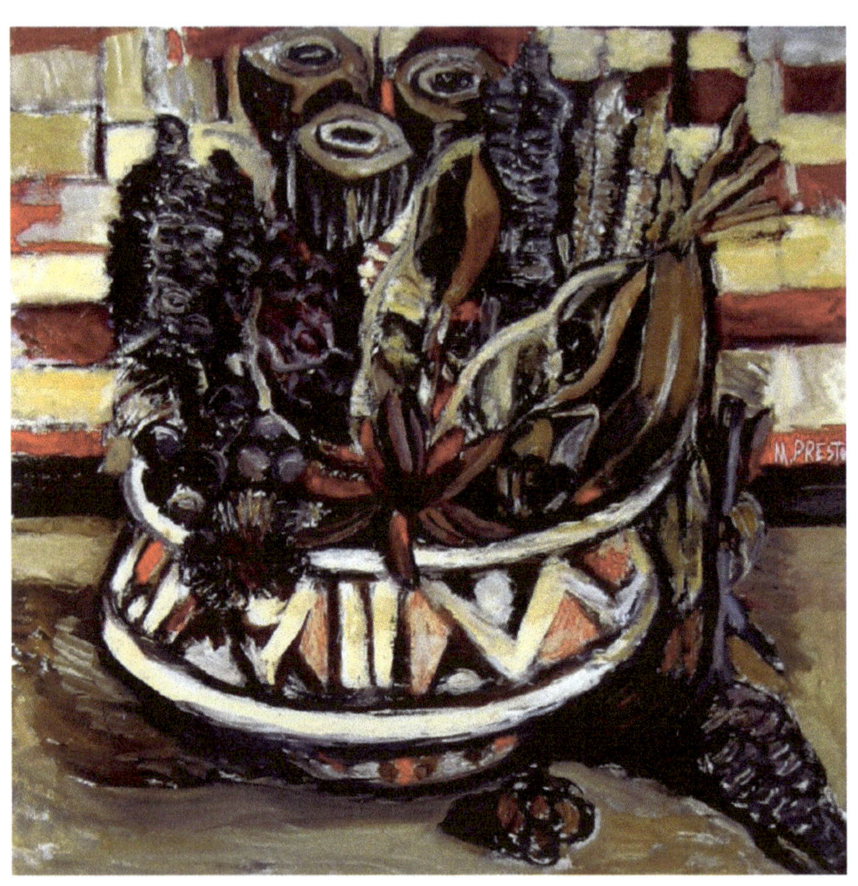

Seed Pods, 1940. Oil. Hand-coloured woodcut.

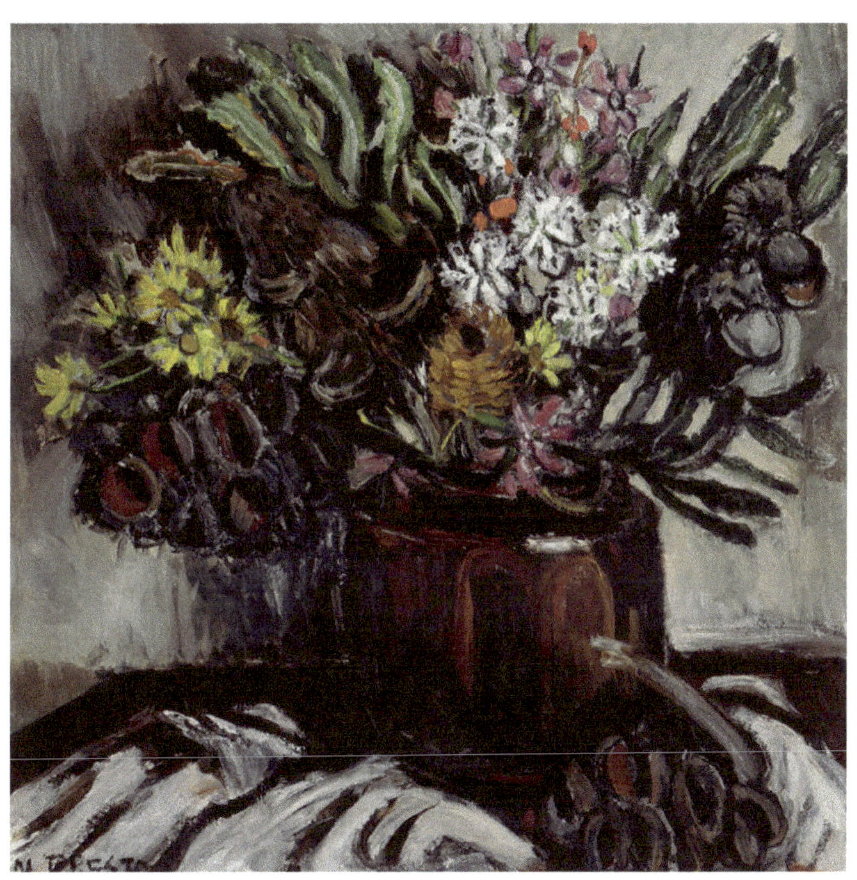

Banksia, 1956. Oil.

sion of the joy of life or aesthetic impulse; it symbolizes the very essence of the spiritual and religious beliefs of the people.'[15] In the foreword to the book, Elkin stresses the fact that design for the Aboriginal people `is used as a language – highly specialized and reverent', a language that reads, to the initiated, as a vital message.

Nicholas Petersen, in Aboriginal Australia, develops this idea of the message, saying:

the simultaneous multiplicity of meanings is central to explaining why art is so important to the people. Through art it is possible to say things that cannot easily be put into words.'[16]

Aboriginal art, he contends, implies, suggests, represents and resonates relationships. Peterson also notes that `the traditional landscape art of the desert peoples is complex in meaning and conceptual', in contrast to the European tradition. These are just the qualities that attracted Preston to Aboriginal art, but, paradoxically, she denies this complexity when she says, in 1930: `We simply cannot get to the bottom of their minds, it is all just a little too simple for us.'[17] She was able to believe that what intrigued her about the mental processes of the `primitive mind' was somehow disconnected from the traditional spiritual beliefs on which those processes were based. `For the student to work from this native art it is necessary that he should try to follow the working of the artist's mental attitude'[19] she advised in 1946, in the same article saying of Aboriginal art:

> if it is used as something from which the essentials of nature and the spirit of the country can be learnt better than from the intellectual achievements of periods of great culture, then it is possible that a beginning can be made for an art for this country that will not be a replica.

She had made the same statement in more general terms in an article of 1928, `Australian Artists Versus Art':[20]

> Until the brain works in conjunction with the spiritual vision, Australian artists will never produce anything different from the work produced in the studios where they learn their trade.

Therefore, while admitting that `art is personal and of the spirit',[21] Preston seems to have been bogged down in the division between mind and spirit that asserted the superiority of science and rationality over traditional systems of belief and spiritual orthodoxy. Furthermore, she seemed to make a distinction between `spirit' and `spiritual'. The quest for `the spirit of the country' was of central importance but was not to be confused, in her opinion, with the spirituality inherent in the totemic aspects of Aboriginal art.

Modernism had celebrated the scientific rational mind as the guiding light. Its interest in primitivism sought to detach primitive art from its sources, an act that became bound up with the exploration of the unconscious mind in Surrealist art and the preoccupation with Jungian archetypes in American Abstract Expressionism. Preston's preoccupation with the analytical aspects of modernism had by this time taken on an almost spiritual purity of intent and in her interpretation of Aboriginal art, she allowed this tendency to dominate.

Many of her statements about `applying' Aboriginal art come down to us today with an unpleasant clang. In 1925, she advised using the designs on Taphoglyphs (sacred tree carvings, indicating a grave) for the making of coverlets that would not `look "beddy", but smart'.[22] The Pikan shield, she avowed, would `make an amusing dado for a child's room' but beware, she said, of using Aboriginal designs on `say, golf or sports stockings' for `the result was fearsome'. Shocking as these observations appear now, they must be seen in context. Alex Barlow, a research officer at the Australian Institute of Aboriginal Studies, feels that it `is greatly to her credit' that she attempted to bring Aboriginal art to the attention of other Australian artists as early as she did, at a time when `Aborigines were still forcibly subdued as uncivilized savages' in many parts of Australia.[23] Her courage and sensitivity in the area is the bright side of what Barlow describes as her attempt `throughout her writings ... to separate that art from its culture, so that its form, its rhythm, its colours and ikons might be used, in isolation from their cultural symbolism.'

Preston's attempt to `apply' Aboriginal art must also be understood in the wider context of her attitude to the applied arts generally. Whenever she thought she was slipping in her art, she went into crafts: woodcuts, monotypes and stencils. Of this work, she commented in 1950: `I find it clears my brain.'[24] In 1925 she cautioned Australians about the need to use Aboriginal art on our own material before some other nation pillaged it. In line with her general beliefs, she said `the beginning should come from the home and domestic arts.'[25] The applied arts were both a testing ground for ideas and a necessary relief from the pressure of her more serious work. Her wide travels would also have awakened her to the value of the native art of individual countries and the equating of golf stockings, cushion covers and table mats with shields, dancing boards and ceremonial carvings, would have seemed to her a logical one. She tended always to reductionism, and this tendency, like most fundamental character traits, proved to be both her great weakness and her great strength.

The sad thing, in many ways, for Preston, was that she did see beyond the surface of Aboriginal art, delighting in the rhythms, the colours, the symbols and the mental processes that informed these elements. `My feeling about Australia is one of sharp forms and dull colours, notwithstanding the blue skies'[26] she said in 1925 in praise of the predominant Aboriginal colours – red, brown and yellow ochre, charcoal and white. She admired `the gumleaf shape of a sharp triangle', the irregularity of Aboriginal design and the austerity of Aboriginal art generally. `It is never repetitive'[27] she said in 1940. `The geometrical designs are balanced, but are never duplicated.' The use of simple, flat colour also greatly appealed to her, placing the emphasis, as it always does, on form.

Through her extensive travels within Australia, Preston became aware of the special characteristics that marked the art of various tribes. With her husband, she travelled widely in search of Aboriginal art forms, making a trip to North Queensland as early as 1927 and a remarkable 15000 kilometre odyssey to Darwin and back in 1947, when she was seventy-two years old. This last trip was made in a utility, but it was only on difficult sections that they hired a mechanic, preferring to travel alone on smoother terrain. Picking up their beef at stations along the way, the indomitable Margaret cooked their meals in a shovel, roasting it in the campfire.

`The fish and plant designs of the Northern Territory and of Arnhem Land are unique',[28] she commented `and the symbolic paintings in caves in the northern Kimberleys are thoughtful and artistic.' But it was the more geometric art of Central Australia, with its widespread use of curvilinear and circular elements that she most admired. `To the European eye', Nicholas Peterson has commented,

> the art of the desert peoples is abstract, geometrical and schematised with its spirals, circles, lines and points but to the Aboriginal eye it stands in a representational relationship to the landscape.[29]

The aim of Synthetic Cubism to create a parallel to (rather than a reflection of) reality by establishing a coded equivalent for every object with a language of visual signs, was thus already realized in Aboriginal art. In Aboriginal art, it came about not as the result of an aesthetic quest but through the need to encode meanings `which endow everyday events and familiar features of the landscape with cosmic significance, by referring to and conjuring up images of the ancestral past.'[30] Hence, its imagery has great potency and has been a repeated attraction for Western artists in the twentieth century, deprived as they are of traditional, ritual and communal beliefs. Painters like John Olsen and Tony Tuckson again picked up on the aesthetic qualities of Aboriginal art in the 1950s, attracted, as Daniel Thomas has noted, by its linear, graphic style: `The spatial effects of white lines floating on dark grounds in ... Oenpelli bark paintings, the rich blackness of charcoal and the extreme sensitivity of drawing.'[31]

Margaret Preston was not simply attracted by the formal qualities of Aboriginal art, despite her statements to the contrary. The distinction she drew between following the Aboriginal artist's mind, while denying the importance of his spirit, was at times not operative. What I am suggesting is that her grasp of the artist's mind at work sometimes did approach a spiritual dimension. Never one to advise others of what she would not do herself she set about exploring some of her theories about Aboriginal art in her own paintings. After her achievements in the realm of still-life, with their exquisite saturated colour, she moved further in the direction of monochrome painting, her geometric still-lifes of 1927 being, in that sense, transitional. By 1935 she was saying:

> Australia is a country that gives the impression of size and neutral colour. To give this impression in canvas or on woodblocks I find it necessary to eliminate `dancing' colour and to heap my light and shadows. I have abandoned the regulation yellow-colour sunlight and made form explain light because I feel that Australia is not a golden-glow

country but a country of harsh, cool light. In my effort to give a feeling of sharp flatness I force my compositions with as much solid light as possible.[32]

The following year the Prestons moved to Stewart Road, Berowra, where they lived in a low wooden house, surrounded by some 5.5 hectares of bushland, a couple of kilometres from the Hawkesbury River. `Its feeling of seclusion is intensified by the smoothly turfed entrance drive which drowns all sounds of approaching wheels,' wrote the Australian Home Beautiful in 1937.[33]

It makes a fitting approach to a garden in which for once our lovely Australian flora is accorded the place of honour ... Margaret Preston's garden is a place of elfin charm and an unspoiled ... wilderness in which there is always something fresh to discover.

It is also reported that Margaret's favourite tree at Berowra was an old banksia, growing in one of the remote corners of the property.

The retreat to Berowra, for three years, from the urban sophistication of Mosman was a significant step for Preston. She was, at this time, midway between the great achievements of her middle age and the creative renewal that would occur in her late sixties. The atmosphere of Berowra, surrounded by the wiry strength of the Australian bush, must also have been permeated by the important concentration of rock engravings that lay nearby in the Sydney, Hawkesbury River district. `Australian landscape and flora are still in the Stone Age', Preston informed the interviewer from the Australian Home Beautiful,

and their real quality can be truly expressed only by artists who are content to tread the primitive paths of their ancestors, see with their eyes and express what they see with patient sincerity.

The Prestons' travels in these years took in the Americas, where Margaret was impressed by the mural art of North America and Mexico. Late in 1938 they were in London, with Margaret studying at the School for Decoration and the following year they returned to Mosman to live. Refreshed and energized by the experience of the bush and the stimulation of extensive travel, she embarked on a series of paintings that express her individual distillation of the many theories she held about Aboriginal art. The Brown Pot, Still-Life – Aboriginal Design, Blue Mountains Theme, Aboriginal Landscape, I Lived at Berowra, Grey Day in the Ranges and Flying Over the Shoalhaven River, were painted within a three-year period. Preston used only the palette of Aboriginal art in these paintings, but they owe at least as much to the Western tradition of landscape painting. She was not an imitator and, in fact, never advocated imitation of Aboriginal art forms. She saw the study of them as a way of clearing the mind and tried to interpret the Aboriginal approach in terms of her own knowledge and experience. 'Knowing the New South Wales Ranges well, I have tried to paint them with stark truth' she wrote in 1941,

> copying the natives in eliminating the western idea of 'time and place'. I am trying to show by form that it is not necessary to rely on colour to suggest any object. I know that art is of the mind and a picture a replica of the mind's vision. A camera-mind produces a camera picture, and this type of mentality has never belonged to the aboriginal.[34]

Her Aboriginal landscapes and still-life are characterized by a simplification of form, an interest in the intervals of the bush (created by dense outlines on rocks and trees) and dots and marks that become a visual shorthand for physical details. As well, she has adopted a more aerial perspective, particularly in Flying Over the Shoalhaven River, with the result that the image becomes a flat pattern on a two-dimensional plane. Of this last painting she wrote, in 1945,

> I have thought, I am flying over the river; the earth was an addition. I concentrated on my clouds, remembering the laws of colour and form; the river the same and lastly the earth.[35]

In this way she tried to simulate the Aboriginal practice of scaling the size or emphasis on elements of a design in order of their importance in the mind of the artist. This can be seen in an Aboriginal illustration of a kangaroo hunt, in which the kangaroo absorbs most of the pictorial space (being the object of principal interest) with the hunter being a tiny, stylized figure by comparison.

Preston also did some Aboriginal-inspired woodcuts in the early 1940s, before largely giving up woodblocking, as too painful to the hands. Some of these woodcuts relate directly to her paintings. The designs of others are influenced by Aboriginal art in a more conventional way, particularly by the X-ray art of Arnhem Land, in which the inner form is revealed within the outline of the animal, fish or reptile. The stick figures of hunters and dancing men, found on rock carvings in this area, are an additional source of inspiration for these woodcuts. Preston also experimented with masonite cuts at this time, employing many of the same themes.

Yale University bought Aboriginal Landscape from a touring exhibition in 1942. The Art Gallery of New South Wales bought three of the others in 1941-42 and Preston's fellow artists were intrigued by the works, although nobody, outside of a few commercial artists, seems to have in any way taken up the challenge of her theories. The critics were not so impressed and predictably it was the Bulletin critic who wrote in 1949:

> She is allowing the aboriginals – a people, as she admits herself, too limited in sensibility and technical capacity to have attempted to paint the wildflowers – to debilitate her talent . . . what is really required is the opposite process – the enrichment of primitive art by the infinitely greater technical and spiritual resources of the civilised artist.[36]

As Alex Barlow points out,

> whilst Preston's attitudes reflect the prevailing attitudes in the 'cultural' and 'educated' circles of her time, they are nowhere as extreme as could be found, especially among people in contact with and in conflict with Aboriginals over land and scarce natural resources.[37]

In 1941 Preston wrote: 'I am humbly trying to follow them in an attempt to know the truth and paint it, and so help to make a national art for Australia.'[38] It was a rare moment of humility on her part but, in all probability, no less sincere for that.

In addition to all her creative work, Margaret Preston continued to write, mostly travel articles for Australia National Journal, and articles on Aboriginal art for Art in Australia and other Ure Smith publications. As well, she gave five major lectures at the Art Gallery of New South Wales (the Carnegie Lectures) in 1938, as part of the sesquicentenary celebrations. The Carnegie Corporation had also given a grant to employ artists as guides on conducted tours of the art gallery for school-children. Dorothy Dundas recounts how she came into one of the old courts of the gallery with her group of school-boys and saw another group gathered like a beehive around a small figure, with reddish, greying hair. The boys were not looking at the paintings, they were looking at Margaret Preston, for that is who it proved to be. 'She just had them spellbound,' said Dorothy. The transcripts of Preston's lectures do not strike much of a chord today but she was an engaging speaker and clearly, it was all in the telling.

In 1942 she shared an exhibition with William Dobell at the Art Gallery of New South Wales and painted, for her, some extraordinary pictures. Japanese Submarine Exhibition, Merry-Go-Round, Charleville, General Post Office, Sydney, and later Tank Traps (1943), and Children's Corner at the Zoo (1944/45) are anomalies in Preston's otherwise logical development. Three of them relate to Australia's wartime situation, while the other two depict children's amusements with a deliberate naivety. It is not difficult to understand her interest in the fragments of Japanese midget submarines, raised from the bottom of Sydney Harbour after their attack on 31 May 1942. Preston was living in Mosman at the time and, like other residents of the harbour suburbs, must have been aware of the searchlights playing across the water after the attack. They were not directed up into the sky, as was usual, but focused down into the depths of the harbour itself. Mrs Jule Lyle, who was living in Vaucluse at the time, remembers the sound of the depth charges which seemed to continue through the night and which cracked all the fine china that her parents had in their cupboards. In Preston's painting, two signs bearing the inscription DO NOT ASK QUESTIONS rest against the submarine pieces and their meaning remains a mystery, for they were not, apparently, in the original display. They may, as Humphrey McQueen suggests in The Black Swan of Trespass, have been an ironic comment on the paranoia with which all things Japanese were viewed during the war. The General Post Office at Martin Place, boarded up with a series of sloping geometric barricades and the prismatic shapes of the tank traps would have appealed to the designer in Preston. The interest in children, even to the adoption of a self-consciously childlike style, may be related to the widespread rediscovery of children's art in the early 1940s.

In 1939 the Department of Education Gallery in Sydney mounted a major international exhibition of children's art. Viktor Lowenfeld's book on the subject, The Nature of Creative Activity, arrived in Australia around 1940 and had a big effect on many artists. The Art in Australia issue of March 1942 carried important articles on the subject by painter Rah Fizelle and by the director of the Museum of Modern Art, Alfred H. Barr. Various influential teachers, from Isabel Mackenzie at the Haberfield Demonstration School to May Marsden at the Sydney Teachers' College were promulgating new methods of teaching children art by `not' teaching them. As well, in 1944, the Sunday Telegraph sponsored a Children's Art Show at the Art Gallery of New South Wales, exhibiting 800 of the 11 296 entries received. Margaret Preston, always responsive to her times, would have been affected by this resurgence of awareness of child art that related to her own knowledge of Roger Fry and Clive Bell's theories on creativity in children.

It is known that the Prestons gave children's parties at Berowra and that Margaret herself seems always to have enjoyed their company. As Ian North notes,[39] the merry-go-round was not a new theme, a woodcut depicting a merry-go-round having appeared in Art in Australia in 1927. Some of these paintings of 1942-46 share stylistic similarities with the Aboriginal landscapes of the same period, particularly in relation to the restricted palette employed. As well, in General Post Office, Sydney, form is defined by a series of marks, lines and strokes characteristic of the Aboriginal-inspired work.

In 1945 the Prestons moved into the Hotel Mosman where they spent the next fourteen years. Vernon Adams interviewed her there for A.M. in 1948 asking:

> `And you a painter of flowers living in a hotel: don't you want a garden?'
>
> `I loathe gardening,' she replied. `I let God make the flowers. I paint them. Here with no house worries I get time to paint.'[40]

The Hotel Mosman was something of an exception for its time. Modern and well situated at Spit Junction, it was virtually the only hotel in the area that offered accommodation, including one suite of rooms, numbers 14 and 15, which the Prestons were to occupy. It was a Toohey's hotel, and as a director of the company, Preston could be assured of the very best service. Wedding receptions and other functions were held there and the hotel kept a very good table. It was on a par with the city hotels at the time and proved to be a place where the Prestons could live comfortably when they were not travelling. Their suite of rooms included a bedroom, a bathroom and one other room, always called Mrs Preston's studio. There was no sitting-room and all meals were had in the dining-room, which, like their suite, was on the first floor of the hotel. Margaret Preston was seventy when they moved in, her husband William, was sixty-four.

`She was delighted with it,' said Dorothy Dundas,

> and Bill was always happy with whatever arrangements she wanted. He never contradicted any of her enthusiasms, but I couldn't help thinking: poor old darling, he must miss having a home.

Barry Lyle was supervising the running of about four hotels at the time and the Hotel Mosman was one of these. He remembers Margaret Preston as a very bombastic woman, aggressive and abrupt. `There was nothing subtle about her' he said. `She was not a snob but she treated the people who worked in the hotel like servants. It was hard to warm to her.'[41] He remembers William Preston as a delightful man, tall, handsome and distinguished. `You could communicate with him,' he said. Lyle recalls them coming back from trips to the Northern Territory, with Margaret dragging in a bag of sand that she would later grind to make pigments. There were other permanent guests at the Hotel Mosman, mostly single ladies, and Margaret often shared morning tea with some of these.

`I think she died with her first shilling' said Lyle, recounting how in the days when rationing was still in force after the war, Margaret would walk out of the dining-room with butter and sugar concealed under her arm. The staff used to make up the Prestons' bedroom but they never touched Margaret's studio which she apparently kept very private. Lyle remembers the Prestons as a very close couple. `They were Darby and Joan,' he said, `and living all the time, as they did, in two rooms.'

William Preston, as Dorothy Dundas has said, obviously enjoyed indulging his wife. `He took tremendous care of her and helped her in every possible way,' Dundas said. `He was very proud of what she did.' Margaret Preston, never one to mince words, remarked in 1948: `I owe everything to Bill.'[42] William Preston, a quiet, very reserved man, must have thrived on his wife's dynamism and extroverted character. He enjoyed their journeys into the outback in search of Aboriginal carvings because, as Margaret put it, `he likes an objective when he drives.'[43] In the A.M. interview she states that she would have given up painting immediately if her husband had ever wanted it. Clearly, however, such an eventuality was never even considered.

`Travelling is what I like best,' Margaret Preston said in 1950.[44]

> Washing up and gardening is what I like least ... But I don't allow my work to interfere with my domestic affairs. I have had a perfectly happy married life and there is only one person in the world – my Bill! I wouldn't dare travel much further than Pymble without him.

It was while they were living at the Hotel Mosman that Preston made yet another fresh start by painting a series of seventy monotypes – prints made by making designs in oil paint or printer's ink on copper plates or sheets of glass, which are then printed either on a press or by rubbing the paper with the heel of the hand – all within a period of six months. Apart from her woodblocking she had also experimented with masonite and linocuts and silk screening. Here was another medium she felt the urge to explore.

In subject matter, Preston's monotypes, which Ure Smith published in book form in 1949, are related to her Aboriginal period – at times in a far more direct way than the paintings. `It must be understood that this work is not copied from the originals,' she said, `but the principles applied.'[45] Many of the monotypes are among the most conventional landscape images Preston produced and, perhaps for this reason, they were very popular. With some exceptions, they still employ the subdued hues of her Aboriginal paintings, but with a luminosity of colour introduced by the printing process. In others, like Bimbowrie Landscape, disconnected anthropomorphic forms hover on a blue ground, which Preston notes, was made from a bush that grew prolifically near the rock painting that had inspired the work. Others of the monotypes were of Australian native flowers, which she again celebrated for their form and colour. `Each flower is individual' she said. `They never respond to being turned into bouquets, as roses and violets do.'[46]

The Bulletin found the wild flower pictures `by far the best'.[47] They disliked her emphasis on the harshness of the bush in the landscapes –

`the lonely and sinister quality of a billabong with its sunken logs; the implacable tangle of branches above the bush track.' Hankering after the lyricism of the Heidelberg School or the golden romance of Hans Heysen, they nonetheless conceded that the monotypes were `stated with an intense emotion, blended from a deep love of the bush with perhaps a deeper storminess of temperament, that makes them, in spite of their harshness, attractive.'

Dorothy Dundas recalls receiving a monotype, hot – or rather wet – off the press. `Mrs Preston wished this to be delivered to you immediately,' the messenger said. `She was very passionate in her enthusiasms,' said Dundas, but it was really a matter of one enthusiasm after another. I remember getting a card from her from Petra, with the rose-red temple. `You must come here at once', it read. `There's nothing in the world like it.' On the next trip, similar sentiments would arrive from Africa.

Preston's last unified phase of work, in 1949 and the early 1950s, centred around stencil prints, many of them with religious themes, interpreted in a characteristically Australian way. Adam and Eve in the Garden of Eden, Golgotha, Noah's Ark, Christ Turning the Water into Wine, and The Expulsion – gouache stencils on black paper – were all completed before 1953. The most obvious explanation for their imagery is that they were done with the Blake Prize in mind. Arrangements for instituting the prize began in 1949, the first one being given in 1951. Established to `bring about a closer cooperation between the church and the artist in the modern world',[48] it was, in the opening, years, regarded as very important. Interest in the art of William Blake himself may have influenced these stencils. It was study of Blake's work that had excited Preston to the possibilities of monotypes in 1946. The treatment of some of the figures in these gouache stencils and some of the overall compositions, particularly The Expulsion, relate to aspects of Blake's style.

`The Blake Prize was something new,' said Treania Smith. `I think it was a challenge to all the artists at the time.' Dorothy Dundas remembers that the Blake Prize motivated a lot of people. `Everyone suddenly felt the urge to paint religious paintings, which had never occurred to them before. It was enormously promoted at the time and enormously prestigious.'

Whatever were the motivations, Preston, with her usual flair, made her religious vision entirely individual. She discussed Adam and Eve in the Garden of Eden with Hal Missingham, casting light on her feelings in the matter. She liked it because it had

> real Australian incident and feeling. The Garden of Eden, obviously here in Australia, the oldest known land of all. Equally obviously, Adam and Eve would be black, our aborigines, with a history stretching back to the dream-time. And our unique and wonderful wild flowers must go in, Sturt's Desert pea, flannel flowers, and the koala, kangaroo, emu and echidna; birds and fish.[49]

She clearly rejoiced in including many of the same creatures in Noah's Ark, just as it is an Aboriginal Adam and Eve who are being expelled from the Garden of Eden in The Expulsion. As well, Christ is turning water into wine outside a good old Australian bush shack, with water tank nearby.

Preston had her last exhibition in 1953 at the Macquarie Galleries, but continued to work up till the late 1950s, some fine woodcuts surviving from this period. During the 1950s, this indomitable woman, then in her late seventies, travelled to some of the most exotic and, for the traveller, challenging places in the world – North Africa, the Middle East and India. In 1959 the Prestons left their `good suburban pub'[50] and moved to a house high up on a hill in Killarney Street, Mosman. There Margaret delighted in her new television set, just as she had once delighted in her `ironing machine', and the latest washing machine. `It is a thing of beauty,' she once remarked of her fridge.[51]

`She had a childish delight in things' Dorothy Dundas commented.

> Knowing her we used to feel – and I know that it's quite against what is being written about her now – that with any interest or enthusiasm she had, it was not necessary for it to be a logical or intellectual thing. If it started her painting, the results were marvellous.

She also continued painting throughout the 1950s, Fish and Black Boys, (Still-Life with National Flowers) and (Still-Life with Bush Flowers in Lustreware Jug) being examples of her output. Fish and Black Boys, 1955, is clearly related to her Aboriginal work of the 1940s, particularly in the treatment of the basket and the heavy black lines that describe the objects. The composition as a whole is far less organized than Preston's earlier paintings, its expressive brushwork and fluid transparencies also linking it to the monotypes of the late 1940s. The other two paintings of Australian wild flowers, including Preston's favourite banksia, show the octogenarian artist still experimenting with cool and warm colour schemes. The orange table of (Still-Life with National Flowers), 1957, is raised to an intensity of hue by the electric blue line that vibrates along its edge and is picked up inside the flower arrangement itself, while (Still-Life with Bush Flowers in Lustreware Jug) is a study in white, grey and dull metallic gold.

What is impressive about these late paintings is not that they may or may not be comparable to her earlier work but that she was able to paint such accomplished pictures at all. Dorothy Dundas remembers that in the last decade of her life Preston showed signs of having lost some of her powers of concentration, and was frequently accompanied by a female companion when she was not with her husband. On one occasion both Dundas and Preston were elected to the Society of Artists hanging committee and Dundas was asked by William Preston to keep an eye on Margaret as he had not been able to get a companion at short notice. The years of commitment gave Preston the instinctive, seasoned ability to continue with her prints and paintings even when her more general powers were deteriorating. That the late works display the artist still engaging with new media and continuing her experimentation with colour is a tribute to her spirit and a blessing conferred by a lifelong dedication to her art.

Margaret Preston died at a private hospital in Mosman on 28 May 1963. Her husband William Preston survived her by thirteen years.

The character of an Individual is not a fixed Property. — T. S. Eliot[52]

Artists are in the business of making ideas visible and as ideas change, or experience informs them with new interpretations or details, so their visual expression shifts – sometimes radically, sometimes almost imperceptibly. Margaret Preston met life head-on, in spite of the `bad growing pains' it gave her, and thus her work is the record of a genuinely creative and adventurous artist. It underwent radical transformations in the shift from realist to Post-Impressionist, to `primitive' in inspiration – so much so that it might seem, at times, to be the work of three different people. Certain points, however, remained stable: principally her ability to hold the viewer within the dynamic design of the picture plane and her unequivocal commitment to the image, which makes her work always a statement, never just a suggestion.

Her dynamic character required many different forms of expression in a career that spanned over seventy years. Her childlike enthusiasm for new ideas and new forms of expression was helped along by a powerful ego, which demanded constant experiment and constant challenge in order that Preston maintain her own high standards of aesthetic commitment. The question of which of her periods is the most successful will be answered by different generations of people according to their individual tastes. Her still-life paintings and wood-cuts of Australian flora and fauna will continue to delight by their freshness, grace and vigour, while the ultimately unresolved spirituality of her Aboriginal-inspired work will also continue to attract and intrigue. As the artist herself said, `The ladder of art lies flat, not vertical.'[53] Her attempts to map out the principles of decorative design in her work were interpreted in a uniquely Australian way, as was her attempt to create a truly indigenous art-form based on Aboriginal art. She was above all, a communicator, not content that art occupy a passive role in people's lives but demanding that it excite, enliven and engage.

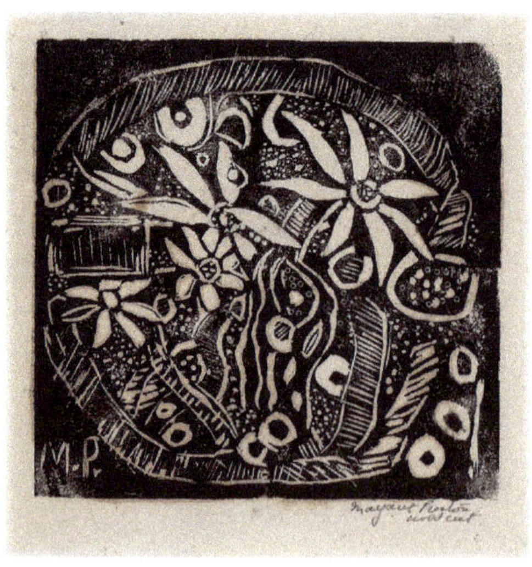

NOTES

INTRODUCTION

1. Margaret Preston. `92 Aphorisms by Margaret Preston and Others'. Margaret Preston: Recent Paintings, edited by Sydney Ure Smith and Leon Gellert. Sydney: Ure Smith 1929. All aphorisms in the text are from this source.

2. Daniel Thomas. `Introduction' in Treania Smith Collection. Sydney: Painters Gallery 1985.

3. Margaret Preston. `Australian Artists Versus Art'. Art in Australia. 3rd Series, no. 26. December 1928.

4. Hal Missingham. `Margaret Preston'. Art and Australia. Vol. 1, no. 2. August 1963.

5. Daniel Thomas. `Introduction'.

6. Margaret Preston. `From Eggs to Electrolux'. Art in Australia – Margaret Preston Number. 3rd Series, no. 22. December 1927.

7. ibid.

8. ibid.

9. ibid.

10. Letter to Norman Carter. MSS 471/1, Mitchell Library, Sydney. Margaret Preston's spelling was often inaccurate and her punctuation non-existent. I have chosen to correct her spelling and add only as much punctuation as will facilitate reading without the loss of her enthusiastic style of writing.

1875-1920

1. Preston's maiden name, McPherson, was also spelt MacPherson, and the spelling will vary according to its most common use at the time.

2. Letter to Norman Carter. MSS 471/1, Mitchell Library, Sydney.

3. Robert Hughes. The Art of Australia. Melbourne: Penguin 1966, p. 121.

4. Margaret Preston. `From Eggs to Electrolux'. Art in Australia – Margaret Preston Number. 3rd Series, no. 22. December 1927. All quotes in the text from `From Eggs to Electrolux' are from this source.

5. Notes by William George Preston. Margaret Preston file, Art Gallery of New South Wales.

6. Margaret Preston. `Why I became a Convert to Modern Art'. The Home. Vol. 4, no. 2. 1 June 1923. All quotes in the text from `Why I became a Convert to Modern Art' are from this source.

7. Margaret Preston. `Away with Poker Worked Kookaburras and Gumleaves!' Sunday Pictorial (Sydney). 6 April 1930.

8. Margaret Preston. `From Eggs to Electrolux'.

9. ibid.

10. ibid.

11. Colin Thiele. Heysen of Hahndorf. Adelaide: Rigby 1969, p. 32.

12. Leon Gellert. `Margaret Preston was One of the Greats'. Sunday Telegraph (Sydney). 8 January 1967.

13. Stella Bowen. Drawn From Life – Reminiscences. London: Collins 1942, p. 18.

14. `The Artist Who Changed Her Name'. Woman's Budget. 16 December 1931.

15. Margaret Preston. `Why I became a Convert to Modern Art'.

16. Gwen Morton Spencer. `Introduction' in Margaret Preston's Monotypes edited by Sydney Ure Smith. Sydney: Ure Smith 1949.

17. Margaret Preston. `Why I became a Convert to Modern Art'.

18. ibid.

19. Margaret Preston. `From Eggs to Electrolux'.

20. `The Artist Who Changed Her Name'. Woman's Budget. 16 December 1931.

21. ibid.

22. Ian North (ed). The Art of Margaret Preston. Adelaide: Art Gallery Board of South Australia 1980, p. 15 (n. 34).

23. Humphrey McQueen interviewed on ABC Radio 2. 31 August 1980.

24. Margaret Preston. `Australia Ahoy!'. Australia National Journal. 1 January 1941, p. 27.

25. Stella Bowen. Drawn From Life. p. 11.

26. ibid., p. 22.

27. ibid., p. 23.

28. ibid.

29. Interview with Mrs Lydia Crawford (niece of Gladys Reynell). 24 May 1985.

30. Letter to Norman Carter. MSS 471/1, Mitchell Library, Sydney.

31. Leon Gellert. `Margaret Preston was One of the Greats'.

32. Letter to Norman Carter (MSS 471/1, Mitchell Library, Sydney) and W.H. Gill (W. H. Gill Papers, Fine Art Society, Melbourne, MSS 285/9, Mitchell Library, Sydney); and W. Ashton (10 April 1941, Margaret Preston file, Art Gallery of New South Wales).

33. The full title of Orpen's painting is Sowing the Seed for the Agriculture and Technical Institution for Ireland (1913).

34. Leon Gellert. `Margaret Preston was One of the Greats'.

35. Margaret Preston. `From Eggs to Electrolux'.

36. Margaret Preston. `Pottery as a Profession'. Art in Australia. 3rd Series, no. 32. June-July 1930.

37. Margaret Preston. `Art for Crafts – Aboriginal Art Artfully Applied'. The Home. Vol 5, no. 5. 1 December 1924, pp. 30-1.

38. Isabelle Anscombe. Omega and After: Bloomsbury and the Decorative Arts. London: Thames and Hudson 1981, p. 16.

39. Roger Fry. `An Essay in Aesthetics'. Vision and Design. London: Oxford University Press 1981, p. 15.

40. Margaret Preston. Transcript of five lectures given at the Art Gallery of New South Wales under the auspices of the Carnegie Corporation of New York Educational Service. Margaret Preston file, Art Gallery of New South Wales. Second lecture, 29 June 1938, p. 4.

41. Isabelle Anscombe. Omega and After. p. 34.

42. William George Preston. Transcript of interview with Hazel de Berg. National Library of Australia, Canberra.

43. Ross McMullin. Will Dyson. Sydney: Angus & Robertson 1984, p. 136.

44. Margaret Preston. `Pottery as a Profession'.

45. Humphrey McQueen. The Black Swan of Trespass. Sydney: Alternative Publishing Cooperative Ltd 1979, p. 151.

46. Interview with Lydia Crawford. 24 May 1985.

47. This painting is now in the collection of the Australian National Gallery.

48. Hal Missingham. `Margaret Preston'. Art and Australia. Vol. 1, no. 2. August 1963.

49. Interview with Dorothy Dundas. 4 May 1985. All further quotes from Mrs Dundas can be attributed to this source.

50. `The Artist Who Changed Her Name'. Woman's Budget. 16 December 1931.

51. Mary Eagle. `Sydney in the 1920s' in Studies in Australian Art, edited by Ann Galbally and Margaret Plant. Melbourne: Department of Fine Arts, University of Melbourne 1978.

1920-1930

1. Lloyd Rees. Peaks and Valleys – An Autobiography. Sydney: William Collins 1985, p. 102.

2. Robert Hughes. The Art of Australia. Melbourne: Penguin 1966, p. 103.

3. Lloyd Rees. Peaks and Valleys. p. 112.

4. Robert Hughes. The Art of Australia. p. 97.

5. Roland Wakelin. 'The Modern Movement in Australia'. Art in Australia, 3rd Series, no. 26. December 1928.

6. William Moore. The Story of Australian Art (2 vols). Sydney: Angus & Robertson 1934, vol. II, p. 104.

7. Cyril Ritchard. 'Art Gallery Trustees – Policy Criticised'. Sydney Morning Herald. 26 October 1933.

8. Margaret Preston. 'Wood-Blocking as a Craft'. Art in Australia. 3rd Series, no. 34. October-November 1930.

9. Joyce Burns Glen. 'Outback Yields Art – Preston Painting Famous'. Christian Science Monitor (Boston). 20 January 1954.

10. 'The "Art" Society – What's Wrong with our Artists?' Truth (Sydney). 15 August 1920.

11. Howard Ashton. 'Two Women Painters'. Sun (Sydney). 17 November 1925.

12. William Moore. 'Blaze of Colour'. Daily Telegraph. 17 November 1925.

13. 'A Late Spring Offering – Thea Proctor and Margaret Preston'. Bulletin. 19 November 1925.

14. 'From an Adelaide Critic'. Bulletin. 16 September 1926.

15. Gavin Long. 'Some Recent Paintings by Margaret Preston'. Art in Australia. 3rd Series, no. 59. May 1935, p. 18.

16. Janine Burke. 'Margaret Preston'. Imprint. (Melbourne). No. 2. 1976.

17. Margaret Preston kept her prices deliberately low, reasoning that she did not need to support herself through their sale. However, this does not explain the enormous disparity between prices of around £400 for major works by artists like Hans Heysen and the average price of around £20 for Margaret Preston's works of the same period.

18. Nicholas Draffin. Australian Woodcuts and Linocuts of the 1920s and 1930s. Melbourne: Sun Academy Series, 1976, p. 7.

19. Margaret Preston. `From Eggs to Electrolux'.

20. Margaret Preston. `Colour'. Art in Australia. 3rd Series, no. 9. October 1924.

21. ibid.

22. Margaret Preston & Thea Proctor. `The Gentle Art of Arranging Flowers'. The Home. Vol. 5, no. 2. 1 June 1924.

23. Letter from Margaret Preston to Hal Missingham, dated 18 May 1959. Margaret Preston file, Art Gallery of New South Wales. The Art Gallery of New South Wales has since restored the work to its original condition.

24. Treania Smith. Treania Smith Collection. Sydney: The Painters Gallery, 1985.

25. Letter from Lionel Lindsay to K. G. Sutton, dated 9 October 1938. MS 8530, La Trobe Library, Melbourne.

26. Letter from Sydney Ure Smith to Hans Heysen dated 22 March 1940. MS 5037, National Library of Australia.

27. Interview with Lloyd Rees. 20 February 1985.

28. Leon Gellert. `Margaret Preston was One of the Greats'. Sunday Telegraph (Sydney). 8 January 1967.

29. Interview with Elaine Haxton. 6 May 1985.

30. Caption to picture in The Home, vol. 5, no. 2, 1 June 1924, p. 2.

31. Interview with Treania Smith. 6 May 1985. All further quotes from Treania Smith can be attributed to this source.

32. Interview with Lloyd Rees. 20 February 1985.

33. W. G. Preston. Transcript of interview with Hazel de Berg. National Library of Australia.

34. Ann Stephen. `Margaret Preston's Second Coming'. Art Network. No. 2. Spring 1980.

35. Ian North (ed.). The Art of Margaret Preston. Adelaide: Art Gallery Board of South Australia 1980, p. 6.

36. Daniel Thomas. `Art Deco in Australia'. Art and Australia. Vol. 9, no. 4. March 1972, pp. 338-51.

37. H. H. Fotheringham. `The Importance of Design and its Relation to the Student'. Art in Australia. 3rd Series, no. 21. September 1927.

38. Thea Proctor. `An Artist's Appreciation of Margaret Preston'. Art in Australia. 3rd Series, no. 22. December 1927.

39. ibid.

40. `Margaret Preston's Two Artistic "Lives"'. Sydney Morning Herald. 3 September 1950.

41. `"I Am Not A Flower" – Mrs. Preston's Art Gallery Portrait'. Sun (Sydney). 6 April 1930.

42. Humphrey McQueen interviewed on ABC Radio 2. 31 August 1980.

43. Hal Missingham. `Margaret Preston'. Art and Australia. Vol. 1 no. 2. August 1963.

44. Gavin Long. `Some Recent Paintings by Margaret Preston'.

1924-1963

1. Margaret Preston. `The Application of Aboriginal Design'. Art in Australia. 3rd Series, no. 31. March 1930.

2. Basil Burdett. `Some Contemporary Australian Artists'. Art in Australia. 3rd Series, no. 29. September 1929.

3. `Creative Art – None in Australia – Mrs. Preston's Opinion'. Sydney Morning Herald. 19 July 1924.

4. Margaret Preston. `Art for Crafts – Aboriginal Art Artfully Applied'. The Home. Vol. 5, no. 5. 1 December 1924.

5. ibid.

6. Stanley Bruce. Mr Bruce on National Objectives (pamphlet). 1925.

7. Margaret Preston. `The Indigenous Art of Australia'. Art in Australia. 3rd Series, no. 11. March 1925.

8. Margaret Preston. `Away with Poker Worked Kookaburras and Gumleaves!' Sunday Pictorial. (Sydney). 6 April 1930.

9. Rex Ingamells. `Jindyworobak'. Chapbook 1 (Adelaide). 1935.

10. Interview with John Winter by Richard King. May 1985.

11. Margaret Preston. `The Indigenous Art of Australia'.

12. Margaret Preston. `New Development in Australian Art'. Australia National Journal. 1 May 1941, pp. 12-13.

13. Margaret Preston. `Away with Poker Worked Kookaburras and Gumleaves!'

14. Margaret Preston. `An Art in the Beginning'. Society of Artists Book 1945-46. Sydney: Ure Smith 1946, pp. 14-15, 19.

15. Margaret Preston. `Meccano as an Ideal'. Manuscripts. No. 2. June 1932, pp. 90-1.

16. F. D. McCarthy. `Introduction' to the sixth edition of Australian Aboriginal Decorative Art. Sydney: Australian Government Printing Service, 1962 (original edition 1938).

17. Nicholas Peterson. `Art of the Desert' in Aboriginal Australia. Sydney: Australia Galleries Directors Council Ltd 1981, p. 46.

18. Margaret Preston. `The Application of Aboriginal Design'.

19. Margaret Preston. `An Art in the Beginning'.

20. Margaret Preston. `Australian Artists Versus Art'. Art in Australia. 3rd Series, no. 26. December 1928.

21. Margaret Preston. `Meccano as an Ideal'.

22. Margaret Preston. `The Indigenous Art of Australia'.

23. Letter from Alex Barlow, Australian Institute of Aboriginal Studies. 14 May 1985.

24. `Distinguished Artist to Show 1953 Work'. Sunday Herald 20 September 1953.

25. Margaret Preston. `The Indigenous Art of Australia'.

26. ibid.

27. Margaret Preston. `Paintings in Arnhem Land'. Art in Australia. 3rd Series, no. 81. November 1940, p. 61.

28. ibid., p. 62.

29. Nicholas Peterson. `Art of the Desert'. p. 44.

30. Howard Morphy. `The Art of Northern Australia' in Aboriginal Australia. Sydney: Australian Gallery Directors Council 1981, p. 65.

31. Daniel Thomas. `Aboriginal Art as Art'. Art and Australia. Vol. 13, no. 3. January-March 1976, p. 281.

32. Gavin Long. `Some Recent Paintings by Margaret Preston'. Art in Australia. 3rd Series, no. 59. May 1935, p. 18.

33. N. Cooper. `Margaret Preston at Home'. The Australian Home Beautiful. 1 February 1937, p. 28.

34. Margaret Preston. `New Development in Australian Art'.

35. Margaret Preston. `An Art in the Beginning'.

36. `The Red Page – Case for the Banksia'. Bulletin. 17 August 1949, p. 2.

37. Letter from Alex Barlow. 14 May 1985.

38. Margaret Preston. `New Development in Australian Art'.

39. Ian North (ed.). The Art of Margaret Preston. Adelaide: Art Gallery Board of South Australia 1980, p. 14.

40. Vernon Adams. `She Has Wanderlust'. A.M. December 1948.

41. Interview with Barry Lyle. 14 May 1985.

42. Vernon Adams. `She Has Wanderlust'.

43. ibid.

44. `Distinguished Artist to Show 1953 Work'. Sunday Herald. 20 September 1953.

45. Margaret Preston. `My Monotypes' in Margaret Preston's Monotypes edited by Ure Smith. Sydney: Ure Smith 1949.

46. ibid.

47. `The Red Page – Case for the Banksia'. Bulletin. 17 August 1949.

48. Alan McCulloch. Encylopedia of Australian Art. Melbourne: Hutchinson, 1984, vol. 2, p. 925.

49. Hal Missingham. `Margaret Preston'. Art and Australia. Vol. 1, no. 2. August 1963.

50. Margaret Preston to Lionel Lindsay. 17 October 1945. MS 9104, La Trobe Library, Melbourne.

51. `Distinguished Artist to Show 1953 Work'. Sunday Herald. 20 September 1953.

52. Margaret Preston used this quotation as the subtitle to her 1923 article `Why I became a Convert to Modern Art'.

53. Margaret Preston. `From Eggs to Electrolux'.

BIBLIOGRAPHY

WORKS BY MARGARET PRESTON

(CHRONOLOGICAL ORDER)

`Why I became a Convert to Modern Art'. The Home. Vol. 4, no. 2. 1 June 1923.

`Colour'. Art in Australia. 3rd Series, no. 9. October 1924.

`Art for Crafts – Aboriginal Art Artfully Applied'. The Home. Vol. 5, no. 5. 1 December 1924.

`The Indigenous Art of Australia'. Art in Australia. 3rd Series, no. 11. March 1925.

`The Best Conditions – For Furnishing the Bedroom, Thereby Providing Some Sound Reasons For Not Sleeping Out'. The Home. Vol. 7. no. 7. 1 July 1926.

`There and Back in Three Months'. The Home. Vol. 7, no. 10. 1 October 1926.

`An Ideal Australian Tour'. The Home. Vol. 7, no. 11. 1 November 1926.

`From Eggs to Electrolux'. Art in Australia – Margaret Preston Number. 3rd Series, no. 22. December 1927.

`New Caledonia and New Hebrides'. The Home. Vol. 9, no. 10. 1 October 1928.

`Australian Artists Versus Art'. Art in Australia. 3rd Series, no. 26. December 1928.

`92 Aphorisms by Margaret Preston and Others' in Margaret Preston: Recent Paintings, edited by Sydney Ure Smith and Leon Gellert. Sydney: Ure Smith 1929.

`The Application of Aboriginal Designs'. Art in Australia. 3rd Series, no. 31. March 1930.

`Pottery as a Profession'. Art in Australia. 3rd Series, no. 32. June-July 1930.

`Away with Poker worked Kookaburras and Gum Leaves!' Sunday Pictorial (Sydney). 6 April 1930.

`Wood-Blocking as a Craft'. Art in Australia. 3rd Series, no. 34. October-November 1930.

`Meccano as an Ideal'. Manuscripts. No. 2. June 1932.

`Basket Weaving for the Amateur'. The Home. Vol. 13, no. 8. 1 August 1932.

`An Exhibition – 1933'. Manuscripts. No. 4. February 1933.

`Just a Tour of the Island'. The Home. Vol. 14, no. 11. 1 November 1933.

`The Puppet Show of Osaka, Japan'. Manuscripts. No. 12. February 1935.

`American Art Under the New Deal – Murals'. Art in Australia. 3rd Series, no. 69. November 1937.

`Running Around the Americas'. The Home. Vol. 18, no. 11. 1 November 1937.

`Crafts that Aid'. Art In Australia. 3rd Series, no. 77. November 1939.

`Some Pioneer Women in Art' in The Peaceful Army – A Memorial to the Pioneer Women of Australia 1788-1938, edited by F. S. Eldershaw. Sydney: Australian Government Printing Service 1939.

`Paintings in Arnhem Land'. Art in Australia. 3rd Series, no. 81. November 1940.

`Australia Ahoy!' Australia National Journal. 1 January 1941.

`O! for Orange'. Australia National Journal. 1 March 1941.

`New Development in Australian Art'. Australia National Journal. 1 May 1941.

`Newcastle of Australia'. Australia National Journal. 1 May 1941.

`Aboriginal Art'. Art in Australia. 4th Series, no. 2. June 1941.

`Tallong Trot'. Australia National Journal. 1 July 1941.

`Aboriginal Art of Australia' in Catalogue of Carnegie Exhibition, 1941.

`Some Aspects of Painting in Australia' in Cultural Cross Section. Adelaide: Jindyworobak 1941.

`The Orientation of Art in the Post-War Pacific' in Society of Artists Book 1942. Sydney: Ure Smith 1942.

`Some Aspects of Contemporary Art'. Meanjin. Vol. 2, no. 1. March 1943.

`Urunga – The Long Beach'. Australia National Journal. February 1944.

`By Punt to Ettalong'. Australia National Journal. July 1944.

`Artists' Groundwork' in Society of Artists Book 1944. Sydney: Ure Smith 1944.

`An Art in the Beginning' in Society of Artists Book 1945-46. Sydney: Ure Smith 1946.

`Some Silk Screen Methods' in Society of Artists Book 1946-47. Sydney: Ure Smith 1947.

`On the Birthday of Jindyworobak' in Jindyworobak Review. Melbourne: Jindyworobak 1948.

`My Monotypes' in Margaret Preston's Monotypes, edited by Sydney Ure Smith. Sydney: Ure Smith 1949.

Preston, M. with Thea Proctor. `The Gentle Art of Arranging Flowers'. The Home. Vol. 5, no. 2. 1 June 1924.

NEWSPAPER ARTICLES

(ARRANGED ALPHABETICALLY BY TITLE)

Some of the sources referred to in this section are: Age (Melbourne), Argus (Melbourne), Advertiser (Adelaide), Daily Telegraph (Sydney), Bulletin (Sydney), Courier (Brisbane), Evening News (Sydney), Mirror (Sydney), Sun Herald (Sydney), Sunday Herald (Sydney).

`A Late Spring Offering – Thea Proctor and Margaret Preston'. Bulletin. 19 November 1925.

`A Note on the Art of Margaret Preston' by Hal Missingham. Sunday Sun Colour Magazine (Sydney). 14 April 1946.

`A Still-Life Show in Sydney'. Bulletin. 23 May 1928.

`Aboriginal Art Influence'. Sydney Morning Herald. 12 August 1941.

`Aboriginal Art is Booming'. Sydney Morning Herald. 30 June 1956.

`An Independent Spirit' by Nancy Borlase. Sydney Morning Herald. 13 September 1980.

`Art and Artists' by William Moore. Courier. 24 September 1927.

`Art Exhibition – Miss Preston's Pictures'. Sydney Morning Herald. 7 August 1929.

`Art Exhibitions – Contemporary Painters'. Sydney Morning Herald. 29 November 1928.

`Art Gallery Purchase'. Sun (Sydney). 1 June 1928.

`Art Gallery Trustees – Policy Criticised'. Sydney Morning Herald. 26 October 1933.

`Art in Arnhem Land – Stone Age Picassos'. Sun Herald. 16 January 1955.

`Art of the Moderns'. Sydney Morning Herald. 9 November 1945.

`Art Students' Exhibition – The Prize Awards'. Age. 19 December 1896.

`Artists Afraid of Revolution'. Mirror. 30 December 1943.

`Artist's Self-Portrait'. Daily Telegraph. 14 April 1930.

`Australian Art Exhibition in London'. Sydney Morning Herald. 26 May 1923.

`Australian Art – Mrs. Preston's Work'. Evening News. 8 August 1929.

`Australian Artists – Successful Exhibitors'. Daily Telegraph. 1 May 1914.

`Australian Flowers – Six Splendid Panels'. Sydney Morning Herald. 11 November 1938.

`Australians at the Salon'. Argus. 7 June 1913.

`Australian Woman Artist Dies'. Sydney Morning Herald. 30 May 1963.

`Big Sydney Show of Paintings' by William Moore. Herald (Melbourne). 7 September 1928.

`Blaze of Colour' by William Moore. Daily Telegraph. 17 November 1925.

`Coloured Print Development' by William Moore. Daily Telegraph. 13 December 1927.

`Contemporary Art in a Buttonhole'. Sunday Sun (Sydney). 25 August 1946.

`Contemporary Group – Annual Art Exhibition'. Sydney Morning Herald. 2 November 1932.

`Contemporary Group – Attractive Exhibition'. Sydney Morning Herald. 10 August 1935.

`Contemporary Group – Fifth Annual Exhibition Macquarie Galleries'. Sydney Morning Herald. 12 November 1930.

`Creative Art – None in Australia – Mrs. Preston's Opinion'. Sydney Morning Herald. 19 July 1924.

`Crucifixion in Art Discussion'. Sunday Herald. 3 September 1950.

`Current Artbursts'. Bulletin. 5 February 1936.

`Distinguished Artist to Show 1953 Work'. Sunday Herald. 20 September 1953.

`Etchers' Work Displayed – Woodcuts by Margaret Preston Show Skill'. Sun (Melbourne). 12 September 1933.

`Exhibition of Margaret Preston's Woodcuts at Dunster Galleries.' Register (Adelaide). 7 September 1926.

`Federal Art Exhibition'. Advertiser. 8 November 1900.

`Flower Painting an art or a Craft' by M. J. McNally. Daily Telegraph. 30 October 1926.

`Flowers Painted to Recipe'. Sydney Morning Herald. 5 October 1944.

`From an Adelaide Critic'. Bulletin. 16 September 1926.

`Gallery "ring" collapses'. Financial Review. 13 June 1980.

`Gallery Trustees "Too Old" – Painter Seeks Spokesman for New Art'. Sydney Morning Herald. 12 October 1940.

`Genius or just great?' by David Dolan. Advertiser. 18 June 1980.

`Great Portrait of Airman – New Exhibition Open to Public'. Sydney Morning Herald. 19 March 1942.

`"I Am Not a Flower" – Mrs. Preston's Art Gallery Portrait'. Sun (Sydney). 6 April 1930.

`Lady de Chair – Views on Art'. Sydney Morning Herald. 8 August 1929.

`Margaret Preston – from eggs to Electrolux' by Alison Fraser. Australian. 24 July 1980.

`Margaret Preston – Give a Vermillion Dog its Due – even if Painted on a Yellow Landscape'. Daily Telegraph. 30 June 1938.

`Margaret Preston was one of the greats' by Leon Gellert. Sunday Telegraph (Sydney). 8 January 1967.

`Margaret Preston's Present Day Art'. Sydney Morning Herald. 22 November 1933.

`Margaret Preston's Two Artistic "Lives"'. Sydney Morning Herald. 3 September 1950.

`Miss R. MacPherson and Miss B. Davidson'. Advertiser. 12 June 1907.

`Modern Art – Is it a Pose?' by George Gadway. Evening News. 30 November 1928.

`Mostly Sydney Exhibitors' by George Bell. Sun (Melbourne). 25 October 1928.

`Mrs Preston's Art – Elaborate Tribute'. Sydney Morning Herald. 20 December 1929.

`Mrs Preston's Paintings – Purchases by National Art Gallery of N.S.W.' Evening News. 15 August 1920.

`New Gallery Exhibition'. Argus. 23 January 1925.

`New Gallery Exhibition' Bulletin. 29 January 1925.

`New Jolt from Margaret Preston' by Humphrey McQueen. National Times. 31 August 1980.

`No "Tourist Art" for Margaret Preston'. Sydney Morning Herald. 22 July 1954.

`One-Woman Art Show – Margaret Preston's Paintings'. Daily Telegraph. 1 August 1929.

`Outback Yields Art – Preston Painting Famous' by Joyce Burns Glen. Christian Science Monitor (Boston). 20 January 1954.

`Preston free of "flower painter" tag' by J. B. Gadson. Bulletin. 23 September 1980.

`Preston the leader' by Robert Rooney. Age. 23 July 1980.

`Purchases for Gallery'. Sydney Morning Herald. 31 March 1942.

`R. MacPherson and G. Reynell at Preece Gallery'. Advertiser. 16 September 1919.

`Society of Artists Annual Exhibition'. Daily Telegraph. 14 September 1923.

`Society of Artists – Spring Show'. Sydney Morning Herald. 11 September 1924.

`Society of Artists – the Modern Influence'. Daily Telegraph. 9 September 1927.

`Still-Life Pictures'. Sydney Morning Herald. 15 May 1928.

`Students at the National Gallery'. Argus. 17 December 1897.

`The "Art" Society – What's Wrong With Our Artists?' Truth (Sydney). 15 August 1920.

`The Contemporary Group – Experiment and Vitality'. Sydney Morning Herald. 14 August 1934.

`The Moderns'. Sun (Sydney). 2 November 1932.

`The Mysterious Life of an Artist'. Sydney Morning Herald. 23 April 1985.

`The Red Page – Case for the Banksia'. Bulletin. 17 August 1949.

`The Students' Exhibition – Conversazione at the Gallery'. Argus. 19 December 1896.

`The Year's Art – Violent Controversies on Significant Developments'. Sydney Morning Herald. 1 January 1934.

`Two Women Artists'. Herald (Melbourne). 23 November 1925.

`Two Women Painters' by Howard Ashton. Sun (Sydney). 17 November 1925.

`Unusual Art – Mrs. Preston's Work'. Sun (Sydney). 7 August 1929.

`US yields a treasure of the past' by Terry Ingram. Financial Review. 28 July 1982.

`Vital Art' by William Moore. Daily Telegraph. 1 December 1927.

`Vitamins at Art Show'. Guardian (Sydney). 7 September 1928.

`W. Ashton and Rose MacPherson given commission by Adelaide Art Gallery'. Advertiser. 4 June 1918.

`Weird Art Will Astound Australia Soon'. Sun (Melbourne). 24 November 1932.

`What Offers? Artists Experiment'. Sun (Sydney). 14 May 1931.

`Woman Artist's Pictures Dynamic'. Mirror. 23 September 1953.

`Women Artists Exhibition'. Bulletin. 27 October 1943.

`Women With Vice-Like Teeth – Critic Finds Modern Art Inhuman, and Praises New Form of Disney'. Daily Telegraph. 21 July 1938.

`Women's Art – Industrial Side'. Sydney Morning Herald. 4 May 1935.

`Women's Painting Impressive'. Sydney Morning Herald. 1 September 1960.

`Woodcuts and Batik'. Sydney Morning Herald. 14 December 1928.

`Woodcuts – Work of Four Artists' by Arthur Streeton. Argus. 1 November 1932.

JOURNAL ARTICLES

Adams, Vernon. `She Has Wanderlust'. A.M. December 1948.

`Australian Woman Artist'. Milady (Perth). Vol. 1, no. 6. December 1948.

Burdett, Basil. `Some Contemporary Australian Artists'. Art in Australia. 3rd Series, no. 29. September 1929.

Burke, Janine. `Margaret Preston'. Imprint (Melbourne). No. 2. 1976.

Cooper, Nora. `Margaret Preston at Home'. The Australian Home Beautiful. 1 February 1937.

`Exhibition at the Grosvenor Galleries'. The Home. Vol. 10, no. 8. 1 August 1929.

Finlayson, R. `Margaret R. MacPherson'. Art in Australia. No. 3. 1917.

`"Flower Piece" – Painted by Margaret Preston'. Bulletin of the National Gallery of South Australia. Vol. 2, no. 3. September 1940.

`"Flowers, Aboriginal Design" – Monotype by Margaret Preston'. Bulletin of the National Gallery of South Australia. Vol. 10, no. 36. April 1949.

Fotheringham, H. H. `The Importance of Design and its Relation to the Student'. Art in Australia. 3rd Series, no. 21. September 1927.

Hutton, G. W. `Margaret Preston's Monotypes'. Meanjin. Vol. 8, no. 4. 1949.

`In Praise of Margaret Preston'. Rydges – Business and Financial Magazine (Sydney). February 1981.

`Influence of Aboriginal Art – Margaret Preston's Paintings'. The Studio. October 1942.

Lake, P. `Four Australian Women Painters'. Refractory Girl. Vol. 8. Autumn 1975.

`"Life's Awkward Moments"'. The Home. Vol. 5, no. 4. 1 September 1924.

Long, Gavin. `Some Recent Paintings by Margaret Preston'. Art in Australia. 3rd Series, no. 59. May 1935.

McQueen, Humphrey. `An Enemy of the Dull'. Hemisphere. Vol. 20, no. 8. August 1976.

Missingham, Hal. `Margaret Preston'. Art and Australia. Vol. 1, no. 2. August 1963.

Missingham, Hal. `Margaret Preston (1883-1963)'. Art Gallery of New South Wales Quarterly. Vol. 5, no. 2. January 1964.

Morgan, E. J. R. `New Painting by Margaret Preston'. Bulletin of the National Gallery of South Australia. Vol. 4, no. 2. February 1943.

Norman, Julie. `Christmas Cards'. Woman. December 1948.

Proctor, Thea. `An Artist's Appreciation of Margaret Preston'. Art in Australia – Margaret Preston Number. 3rd Series, no. 22. December 1927.

Radcliffe-Brown, A. `Margaret Preston and Transition'. Art in Australia – Margaret Preston Number. 3rd Series, no. 22. December 1927.

Reed, John. `"Australian Present-Day Art"'. Angry Penguins, Autumn 1944.

Smith, Sydney Ure. `Editorial'. Art in Australia. No. 11. 1921.

Smith, Sydney Ure. `Editorial'. Art in Australia – Margaret Preston Number. 3rd Series no. 22. December 1927.

Smith, Sydney Ure. `The Revival of the Woodcut'. Art in Australia. 3rd Series, no. 4. May 1923.

Stephen, Ann. `Margaret Preston's Second Coming'. Art Network. No. 2. Spring 1980.

`The Artist Who Changed Her Name'. Woman's Budget. 16 December 1931.

Thomas, Daniel. `Aboriginal Art as Art'. Art and Australia. Vol. 13, no. 3. January-March 1976.

Thomas, Daniel. `Art Deco in Australia'. Art and Australia. Vol. 9, no. 4. March 1972.

Wakelin, Roland. `Contemporary Art' in Jubilee Exhibition of Australian Art. Sydney: Ure Smith 1951.

Wakelin, Roland. `Post Impressionism in Sydney, Some Personal Recollections'. Art Gallery of New South Wales Quarterly. Vol. 3, no. 2. January 1962.

Wakelin, Roland. `The Modern Movement in Australia'. Art in Australia. 3rd Series, no. 26. December 1928.

`What Do We Want For The New Year?' Woman. 5 January 1953.

`What is Modern Painting?' Country Art Exhibitions Catalogue – Second Series 1945-46. Sydney: National Art Gallery of New South Wales 1946.

Wilkinson, Kenneth. `Contemporary Art Arrives'. Art in Australia. 3rd Series, no. 81. November 1940.

BOOKS AND MONOGRAPHS

Australian Gallery Directors Council. Aboriginal Australia. AGDC 1981.

Anscombe, I. Omega and After – Bloomsbury and the Decorative Arts. London: Thames & Hudson 1981.

Biven, R. Some Forgotten ... Some Remembered (Women Artists of South Australia). Adelaide: Sydenham Gallery 1976.

Bowen, S. Drawn from Life – Reminiscences. London: Collins 1942.

Burke, J. Australian Women Artists 1840- 1940. Melbourne: Greenhouse 1980.

Butler, R. The Prints of Margaret Preston: A Catalogue Raisonne. Melbourne: Australian National Gallery/Oxford University Press 1987

Catalano, G. The Years of Hope: Australian Art and Criticism 1959-1968. Melbourne: Oxford University Press 1981.

Deutscher, C., R. Butler and D. A. Witt. Survey of Australian Relief Prints 1900-50. Melbourne: Deutscher Galleries 1978.

Draffin, N. Australian Woodcuts and Linocuts of the 1920s and 1930s. Melbourne: Sun Academy Series 1976.

Edwards, D. & Peel, R. Margaret Preston. Sydney, Art Gallery of New South Wales 2005

Fry, R. Vision and Design. London: Oxford University Press 1981.

Galbally, A. and M. Plant (eds). Studies in Australian Art. Melbourne: Department of Fine Arts, University of Melbourne 1978.

Gleeson, J. Modern Painters 1931-1970. Sydney: Landsdowne Press 1971.

Gombrich, E. H. The Sense of Order – A Study in the Psychology of Decorative Art. Oxford: Phaidon 1979.

Haese, R. Rebels and Precursors. Melbourne: Allen Lane 1981.

Horton, M. (ed). Present Day Art in Australia. Sydney: Ure Smith 1969.

Hughes, R. The Art of Australia. Melbourne: Penguin Books 1966.

Lindsay, L. Addled Art. Sydney: Angus & Robertson 1942.

McCarthy, F. D. Australian Aboriginal Decorative Art. Sydney: Trustees of the Australian Museum 1938.

McCulloch, A. Encyclopedia of Australian Art. Melbourne: Hutchinson 1984.

McQueen, H. The Black Swan of Trespass. Sydney: Alternative Publishing Cooperative Ltd 1979.

Moore, W. The Story of Australian Art (2 vols). Sydney: Angus & Robertson 1934.

Mountford, C. P. Aboriginal Art. Melbourne: Longmans 1961.

North, I. (ed.). The Art of Margaret Preston. Adelaide: Art Gallery Board of South Australia 1980.

Radford, R. Outline of Australian Printmaking. Ballarat: Ballarat Fine Art Gallery 1976.

Rees, L. Peaks and Valleys – An Autobiography. Sydney: William Collins 1985.

Rees, L. Small Treasures of a Lifetime. Sydney: William Collins 1984.

Smith, B. Australian Painting 1788-1970. Melbourne: Oxford University Press 1971.

Smith, T. Treania Smith Collection. Sydney: Painters Gallery 1985.

Smith, Sydney Ure. Australian Art Annual 1939. Sydney: Ure Smith 1939.

––, Margaret Preston's Monotypes. Sydney: Ure Smith 1949.

––, Present Day Art in Australia. Sydney: Ure Smith 1943.

––, Present Day Art in Australia. Sydney: Ure Smith 1945.

––, Present Day Art in Australia. Sydney: Ure Smith 1949.

--, Society of Artists Book 1942. Sydney: Ure Smith 1942.

--, Society of Artists Book 1944. Sydney: Ure Smith 1944.

--, Society of Artists Book 1945-46. Sydney: Ure Smith 1945-46.

Smith, Sydney Ure and J. Burke (eds). Art and Design. Sydney: Ure Smith 1949.

Smith, Sydney Ure and L. Gellert (eds). Margaret Preston – Recent Paintings 1929. Sydney: Art in Australia 1929.

Thiele, C. Heysen of Hahndorf. Adelaide: Rigby 1969.

Thomas, D. Outlines of Australian Art – The Joseph Brown Collection. Melbourne: Macmillan 1973.

UNPUBLISHED WORKS

Carter, Norman. Letters received – February 1902-June 1961. Mitchell Library, Sydney. MSS 471/1.

North, Ian, Isobel Seivl and Humphrey McQueen. Transcript of interview, ABC Radio 2. 31 August 1980 (Peter Morton).

Preston, Margaret. Transcript of five lectures given at the Art Gallery of New South Wales under the auspices of the Carnegie Corporation of New York Educational Service – 22 June; 29 June; 6 July; 15 July; 20 July 1938. Margaret Preston file, Art Gallery of New South Wales.

Preston, William George. Transcript of interview with Hazel de Berg. National Library of Australia, Canberra.

W. H. Gill Papers. Fine Art Society, Melbourne. Mitchell Library, Sydney. MSS 285/9.

INDEX

ACKNOWLEDGMENTS

The original editions of this book acted as a catalogue for the Margaret Preston exhibition at the Art Gallery of New South Wales in 1985, thanks to Brian Johns and the creative team at Penguin Books. My thanks to the AGNSW staff, especially the director Edmund Capon, Anna Waldmann and Nicholas Draffin. I thank Alex Barlow and Warwick Dix at the Australian Institute of Aboriginal Studies for their interest and advice, and Grace Butel for her diligent and tireless research. Lloyd Rees, Lydia Crawford, Dorothy Dundas, Treania Smith, Elaine Haxton, Jule and Barry Lyle all were most generous with their time to discuss their meetings with the artist. William Collins gave kind permission to use excerpts from Peaks and Valleys by Lloyd Rees, and Drawn From Life by Stella Bowen. Thames & Hudson gave kind permission to use excerpts from Omega and After by Isabelle Anscombe. I would also like to thank Art and Australia, the Bulletin, the State Library of New South Wales and the Sunday Telegraph.

www.ingramcontent.com/pod-product-compliance
Lightning Source LLC
LaVergne TN
LVHW052347100826
845147LV00012B/772
9781925416015